Peter P. Clark

STRUCTURAL VISUALIZATION

BY

JOHNSON O'CONNOR

HUMAN ENGINEERING LABORATORY

INCORPORATED

STRUCTURAL VISUALIZATION

| First Edition | 1943 | 20,000 copies |
| Second Edition | 1953 | 20,000 copies |

This brochure replaces

CHARACTERISTICS COMMON TO ENGINEERING
EXECUTIVES

published

First Edition	First Printing	1935	500 copies
First Edition	Second Printing	1936	300 copies
Second Edition	First Printing	1937	300 copies
Second Edition	Second Printing	1937	500 copies
Third Edition	First Printing	1938	5000 copies

JOHNSON O'CONNOR RESEARCH FOUNDATION INCORPORATED
11 East Sixty Second Street New York 21 New York
(Formerly at Stevens Institute of Technology Hoboken New Jersey)

HUMAN ENGINEERING LABORATORY INCORPORATED
347 Beacon Street Boston 16 Massachusetts
(Formerly at 381 Beacon Street)

HUMAN ENGINEERING LABORATORY
2012 Delancey Place Philadelphia 3 Pennsylvania
(Formerly at Chestnut Hill Academy)

161 East Erie Street Chicago 11 Illinois
(Formerly at Illinois Institute of Technology
Glessner House 1800 Prairie Avenue)

15 West Ninth Street Tulsa 3 Oklahoma
(Formerly at 1403 Riverside Drive)

657 Fifth Avenue Fort Worth 4 Texas
(Formerly at 1409 Sinclair Building)

302 South Bunker Hill Avenue Los Angeles 17 California
(Formerly at Park View Building 2404 West Seventh Street)

CONTENTS

TABLES

FIGURES

WORKSAMPLES

An eager schoolboy occasionally tries a temporary job each vacation, hoping to judge more intelligently whether or not to continue in that vocational quarter for life. One summer he runs errands for an architectural firm or files blueprints. The next he washes floors in a private hospital to sense the medical world at close range. A third, he checks machine-wrapped cakes conveyed before him in a modern soap factory. But even so catholic an experiential range yields little insight into advertising, banking, certified public accounting, executive work, diplomacy, insurance, law, scientific research, or a host of potential futures. Furthermore prolonged weeks of errand running and blueprint lettering do not touch the creative throes of the architectural profession. Several summers in a busy hospital may not reveal the doctor's mind or disclose inspiring public-health problems. But could the real essence of each occupational realm be distilled and freed from extraneous factors, then might a boy try a great variety in a short time.

With this aim the Human Engineering Laboratory undertook some twenty years ago to construct a series of concentrated WORKSAMPLES. The procedure in building the structural sample involved asking a number of recognized engineers of known accomplishments to try a simple, standardized task under rigidly controlled conditions, and recording the outcome. In the first instance engineers finished no more rapidly or accurately than clerks, accountants, production followers, and the general run of applicants for factory jobs, showing the task to fail in its purpose, for the mere wish for a fair sample does not prove the significance of the result. Successful engineers later tried a second, differently designed sample but still did no better. After some thirty-five or forty attempts the staff stumbled on a mechanical puzzle, now called the wiggly block, which engineers of standing solve more quickly than men and women in general. Today a boy who does the wiggly block rapidly displays a gift in common with successful engineers; speed of performance indicates the effective operation of a trait more typical of engineers than of the general public.

This demonstrated excellence may be either natural or acquired. Professional engineers may excel because of their technical knowledge, practical experience, and acquired skill, or because of some instinctive feeling for the work; and the Laboratory wished to distinguish professional training, which anyone may acquire, from an inherent gift, which determines the general direction for setting out.

Of one hundred boys who some twelve years ago graded A, in the top quarter for their age, in this engineering sample, seventy entered some aspect of engineering and earned their living in the field five years or longer. Of one hundred who, at the same time, graded B, thirty remained in engineering equally long; of one hundred C's, ten; of one hundred D's, two. Compared with others, the chances in engineering of the boy who grades D are two in one hundred, for these two grade-D boys became ultimately as successful as the seventy A's. For one who grades C the computed chances are ten in one hundred; B, thirty in one hundred, compared with the boy who grades A in the standardized wiggly block whose chances in engineering are seventy in one hundred.

A low score in the wiggly block gives cause for hesitation, but should not stop one despotically, for performance of any sample is no final answer, rather a bit of concrete information to include in the consideration of the future. A boy may grade D and justly enter engineering, recognizing his statistical chances as two in a hundred, but with the belief that other factors, interest, opportunity, necessity, outweigh this finding.

Even to the boy who grades high the staff cannot justifiably say: 'You should be an engineer', for the comparatively few surgeons who try the task score high. Skilled mechanics and machine setup men score equally high. Architects score high, as do also draftsmen, cytologists, physicists, astronomers, stage designers, and laboratory technicians.

Diemakers and toolmakers, aristocrats of the mechanical world, picture to themselves inside a rough casting or rectangular metal block the finished solid product portrayed by white lines on a blueprint. Architects see in their mind's eye the proposed building shown on working drawings. Cytologists study under the microscope, not the entire cell, but thin sections, and from these build the three-dimensional concept. Surgeons delve confidently into solid tissues where an error in depth may mean death. Representatives of many occupations where survival demands the unerring visualization of solid structures score high in this early worksample, which thus becomes no longer a sample of engineering, or of any restricted job, but of a manner of thinking which enters many fields.

The astonishing discovery resolves a doubt which early troubled the staff. With more than twenty thousand jobs now listed, the original aim required as many distinct tests, a blatantly impractical proceeding, for could a boy try a fresh one every ten minutes he would consume several years in trying them all, and otherwise would never know which he might do best. With the new finding a boy who performs poorly a specific activity may eliminate from consideration all work into which that activity enters as a major factor.

From the industrial viewpoint, seeking an available workman for a determinate operation, the idea of a sample, so simple that it can be given in the employment office, seems at first glance the expedient procedure. For a stationary organization, which foresees no changes, no improvements, no promotions, this may hold true. Such a sample shows fitness or unfitness for the original, but gives no insight into qualifications for anything else; and men are not static, they cannot be put into little compartments to remain there indefinitely. They are alive, developing organisms. Men must be helped to improve, to do better work. They must occasionally be promoted. They must often be shifted from one duty to another as the public alters its demand. The sample of an activity which enters many fields shows a man's possibilities for a large group of jobs, for all jobs which can be classified as requiring that activity or as not requiring it.

Because the Laboratory's worksamples measure elemental activities rather than temporal occupations one must use them with scrupulous care, not as sample jobs, but as aids in analyzing one's opportunities, ambitions, difficulties, in terms of one's own measured strengths and indicated limitations. This imposes ripe insight on those who interpret test results. No longer does the awaited outcome relegate one enduringly to an established occupational area.

With the abandonment of the job as the criterion against which to check each incipient test, the Laboratory needed another standard amounting to a new philosophy. It assumed, as an operating hypothesis, the existence of inherent, statistically independent, unit characteristics, mental elements as real and scientifically measurable as the chemical elements: hydrogen, chlorine, oxygen, and the like. The gradual isolation of the latter led to a constantly widening science of chemistry. The early assumption of mental elements has led to the construction of thirteen separate, exclusive, nearly non-correlating tests, each with its own known accuracy great enough to prove beyond argument that it approximates something, uninfluenced by the remaining dozen. There exist at least thirteen prime ways of thinking; each plays its part in many types of work.

In some of the thirteen, men collectively excel women; in others, women excel men. But a majority share no sex distinction. Some improve rapidly with age and mature early, others more slowly, still others seem nearly mature at the earliest age at which the Laboratory can test, age nine. Several mature three and four years earlier with girls than with boys. Those which mature late drop slightly with inevitable age after thirty-five or forty.

These mathematically distinct traits combine in more than eight thousand different ways so that with thirteen tests, which the Laboratory can administer in six hours, in two appointments of three hours each, it separates eight thousand different types of persons and distinguishes the requirements of eight thousand different jobs. Thus, in place of trying eight thousand samples, one for each job, a boy may now try, in about one five hundredth of the time that would take, thirteen samples of thirteen ways of thinking and when through, by combining them mathematically, get some notion of his chances of success in eight thousand vocational directions.

This brochure discusses each of these thirteen separate characteristics. The boy who possesses but one has little trouble in using it. He goes directly ahead, often making a far more outstanding place for himself in the world of affairs than a boy more gifted; for although occasionally two traits work easily together and point in a clearly defined direction, at other times the Laboratory knows of no stable task which demands a peculiar combination of two, three, four, or more traits.

Furthermore, the familiar chemical compound called WATER (H_2O) does not resemble either of its two ingredients, hydrogen and oxygen, and would never have been predicted from an intimate knowledge of these separate substances. Similarly a combination of two aptitudes may not be what one would expect from a knowledge of the two separately. Gradually the Laboratory will study not only each isolated aptitude but every possible combination. This means eight thousand research studies, an enormous task. Meanwhile each individual must accept his own esoteric combination of aptitudes as a personal responsibility which he must discharge.

II

STRUCTURAL VISUALIZATION

Measured less accurately than most aptitudes, structural visualization holds so significant a role in mechanized civilization that interpretations of results bear heavily on the characteristic. But the unmistakable presence of the trait does not settle with clear-cut finality the irrevocable choice between a technical school and arts college. The structurally-minded boy obtains excellent science courses in many general universities, or completes equally well the daily assignments in technical and engineering institutions, granted always his qualifications given later under accounting aptitude and English vocabulary.

Because of the inaccuracies of our measuring instruments, the boy who scores neither high nor low may encounter no trouble with engineering traceable to this lack, or may fail as completely as one who, without good luck, scores low in the test. In face of this uncertainty, a boy interested in engineering, who grades B in structural visualization, should take science courses in a general college or enter an engineering school associated with a university where, if engineering proves less

FIGURE 2

BOYS HIGH IN STRUCTURAL VISUALIZATION SUCCEED IN ENGINEERING SCHOOL

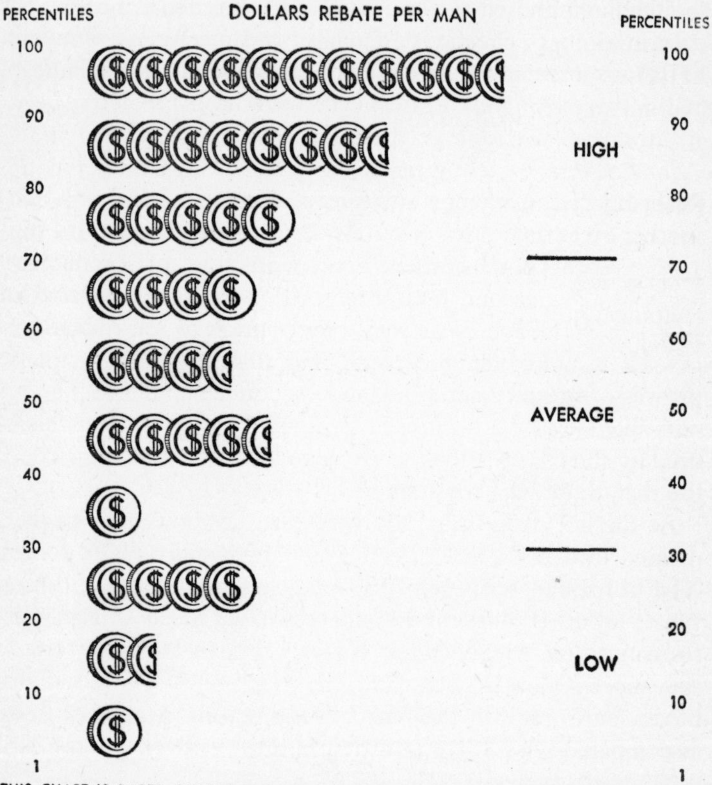

THIS CHART IS BASED ON 298 ENGINEERING-SCHOOL STUDENTS TESTED AS UNDERGRADU-
ATES AT STEVENS INSTITUTE OF TECHNOLOGY. THE TOP 32 IN WIGGLY-BLOCK SCORES
EARNED A TOTAL OF $3350 IN TUITION REBATES AWARDED FOR A COMBINATION OF HIGH
SCHOLARSHIP AND NOTABLE EXTRA-CURRICULAR ACTIVITIES. THIS EQUALS APPROXIMATELY
$105 PER MAN, REPRESENTED BY THE HORIZONTAL ROW, AT THE TOP, OF TEN AND ONE
HALF SYMBOLS EACH OF WHICH STANDS FOR TEN DOLLARS. THE BOTTOM 31 MEN IN
WIGGLY-BLOCK SCORES EARNED A TOTAL OF ONLY $250, AWARDED IN THE SAME MANNER,
OR LESS THAN TEN DOLLARS PER MAN SHOWN BY THE LONE SYMBOL AT THE BOTTOM.

attractive than anticipated, he can shift to academic subjects
without breaking college ties and losing budding friendships.

The high-school boy unquestionably low in structural visualization should not ordinarily enter an engineering or exclu-

sively scientific school, for he finds both analytical geometry and college physics, to name but two technical subjects required by most such institutions, troublesome and often unprofitable. In a liberal-arts college the non-structural boy should limit himself to one laboratory science annually, for even in biology, chemistry, geology, and mechanical drawing, he labors disproportionately hard to overcome his handicap.

I

Realizing that, while one boy devotes himself wholly to books, another gives time to extra-curricular activities, and a third supports himself, Stevens Institute of Technology at one time attempted a financial appraisal of each boy's total contribution to the educational community, including classroom marks, athletic prowess, fraternity activities, and executive functions. The results suggest that boys low in structural visualization, as measured by the wiggly block, contribute less to engineering-school life than those who score high.

SUCCESS IN
ENGINEERING
SCHOOL

At the left of figure 2, the vertical scale shows 298 students divided into ten equal groups based on wiggly-block scores. The horizontal scale gives the corresponding average tuition rebate awarded outstanding underclassmen, based on total performance. As wiggly-block scores improve from bottom to top, success increases steadily. The 31 students whose wiggly-block scores rank in the bottom tenth earned a total of $250, as compared with $3350 awarded to those in the top tenth.

2

The Century Dictionary defines ENGINEERING as: 'The art of constructing and using engines or machines', and calls an ENGINE: 'An apparatus for producing some mechanical effect; a skilful mechanical contrivance'. This leaves vague and uncertain boundaries, but excludes some activities, perhaps teaching, politics, diplomacy, law, insurance, banking, accounting, and the like. Forty-seven accountants, with an

STRUCTURAL
VISUALIZATION
AND ENGINEERING

FIGURE 3

ACCOUNTANTS AND TEACHERS AVERAGE LOW IN STRUCTURAL VISUALIZATION
ENGINEERS AND METALLURGISTS AVERAGE HIGH

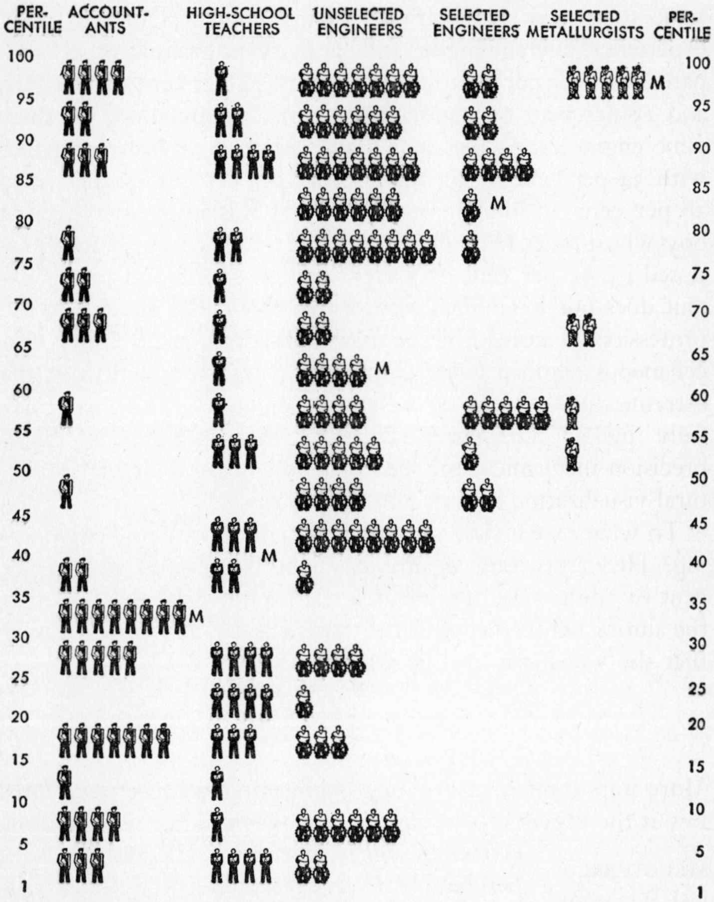

EACH SYMBOL REPRESENTS AN ACTUAL SCORE
M LOCATES THE MEDIAN OF EACH GROUP

IN STRUCTURAL VISUALIZATION, WORKSAMPLE 5, 47 ACCOUNTANTS SCATTER FROM BOTTOM TO TOP BUT AVERAGE LOW (32nd PERCENTILE); 38 HIGH-SCHOOL TEACHERS ALSO SCATTER BUT AVERAGE HIGHER (40th PERCENTILE); 80 ENGINEERS OF ALL TYPES FROM MANY COMPANIES AVERAGE STILL HIGHER (62nd PERCENTILE); 18 DESIGNING AND RESEARCH ENGINEERS, AND 9 METALLURGISTS, AT THE EXTREME RIGHT, AVERAGE STILL HIGHER.

average of ten years' experience, score low in structural visualization, as measured by the wiggly block and shown at the left of figure 3. (See Technical Report 81, page 26, for details.) Further to the right in the same figure, thirty-eight high-school teachers score slightly higher but still as a group low in the same structural characteristic. Eighty engineers of ten years' experience, average higher still, 42 per cent grading *A*, as compared with 21 per cent of accountants, 24 per cent of teachers, and 25 per cent of a miscellaneous male population. Of these same engineers, 64 per cent grade either *A* or *B* as compared with 34 per cent of accountants, 42 per cent of teachers, and 50 per cent of adult males. Accepting this study as typical, a boy who grades *C* or *D* in the wiggly block lacks a trait possessed by 64 per cent of present-day engineers and to this extent does not resemble a majority of those who survive in the profession. If instead of the middle distribution of eighty miscellaneous engineers one consider the fourth and fifth at the extreme right, based on designing engineers with two carefully picked, eminently successful manufacturers of high-precision mechanical and electrical apparatus, their high structural visualization is even more obvious.

To what extent should a boy who scores low avoid engineering? He may create an unusual niche for himself and 36 per cent of adults who survive lack the trait. But he should know the duties before he ventures, regard a low score as warning that the work may not be what he expects.

3

More important than avoiding engineering because one scores low is the urgency of using the trait when high, for numerous evidences suggest that every idle aptitude adds perceptibly to one's chances of financial failure. Were the characteristic merely unnecessary in non-structural activities, successful men in accounting should grade roughly half above average, half beneath, instead of low. To some extent, high-scoring men turn to engineering, architecture, surgery, and the like, leaving the remainder for non-structural occupations, a statistical

STRUCTURAL
VISUALIZATION
AND BANKING

FIGURE 4

MORE STRUCTURAL VISUALIZATION THAN ACCOUNTING APTITUDE MEANS FAILURE IN BANKING

SIX INDIVIDUALS

PER-CENTILE	I	II	III	IV	V	VI	PER-CENTILE
100	Structural Visualization		Structural Visualization				100
90				Structural Visualization			90
80		Structural Visualization		Accounting Aptitude	Accounting Aptitude	Structural Visualization	80
70			Accounting Aptitude		Accounting Aptitude		70
60	Accounting Aptitude	Accounting Aptitude					60
50							50
40						Accounting Aptitude	40
30							30
20							20
10							10
1						Structural Visualization	1

THIS FIGURE SHOWS THE RELATIVE STRUCTURAL VISUALIZATION AND ACCOUNTING APTITUDE OF SIX COLLEGE MEN WHO ENTERED BANKING. INDIVIDUALS I TO V FAILED. ALL SCORE HIGHER IN STRUCTURAL VISUALIZATION THAN IN ACCOUNTING APTITUDE. INDIVIDUAL VI, AT THE EXTREME RIGHT, SCORES LOWER THAN THE OTHERS IN ACCOUNTING APTITUDE BUT HIGHER IN THIS THAN IN STRUCTURAL VISUALIZATION. HE SUCCEEDED IN BANKING.

explanation; but also high-scoring individuals who try non-structural fields fail to survive.

On entering a bank, six college graduates scored as tabulated schematically in figure 4. With the first five structural visualization exceeds accounting aptitude and all left banking within two years. Case 1 scores at the sixtieth percentile in accounting aptitude, but still higher, at the one hundredth percentile, in structural visualization. Case II scores at the sixtieth percentile in accounting aptitude but again higher in structural visualization. Case VI, who remained and succeeded, scores lower in accounting aptitude, essential to banking, than any of the other five, but higher in this trait than in others.

Another high-structural man, above the ninetieth percentile, started in a local savings bank as a sixteen-year-old messenger boy. In some twelve years he climbed, by unbroken effort, to the rank of treasurer; and then lost the position apparently through no assignable fault of his own. Due to his unimpeachable service record he became controller for a small factory, but at the end of another decade lost this, again through a combination of seemingly unavoidable circumstances. At this point he came to the Laboratory to be tested and with no effort scored notably high in structural visualization. At first he disclaimed any technical engineering interest, knew nothing of either physics or chemistry; but bit by bit it transpired that purely as a pastime he directed weekends a congenial band of associates in a construction project of sufficient scope to have been reported in New York newspapers and national magazines. Whether or not the time thus consumed detracted from his main vocation is now difficult to say; but he had never faced the reason for enjoying his building hobby, and ignored blindly every natural chance of applying his structural visualization to his remunerative task. He would certainly have been more valuable to a manufacturing employer and probably a better adjusted human being could he have used this additional aptitude the major portion of the working day rather than exerting it free weekends only.

Cost accountants, estimators, and those making material surveys, borderline activities between banking and engineering, obviously need structural visualization and accounting aptitude. One engineering-school graduate, with this pair, holds a special place in the heart of the banking world as a full-time technical adviser. He travels over the globe investigating engineering enterprises and surveying manufacturing plants applying for loans, visits factories whose income depends principally upon mechanical treatments, evaluates their equipment, and occasionally suggests improvements. Another man,

with no formal engineering education but equally high structural visualization, performs much the same service for a
broker handling blocks of non-listed stocks.

In theory the ideal banking pattern includes high accounting aptitude, perhaps even in the top ten per cent, and low
structural visualization, in the bottom half (table 1), but in

TABLE I

CHARACTERISTICS COMMON TO EIGHTY BANK EMPLOYEES

TRAIT	RATING
ACCOUNTING APTITUDE (WORKSAMPLE 1)	VERY HIGH (MEN'S NORMS)
ACCOUNTING APTITUDE (WORKSAMPLE 268)	VERY HIGH (MEN'S NORMS)
PERSONALITY	NOT EXTREMELY SUBJECTIVE
STRUCTURAL VISUALIZATION	BELOW AVERAGE (MEN'S NORMS)

Tellers

FINGER DEXTERITY	HIGH

actual practice no sharp rule distinguishes those who belong
in this work, success often depending more directly upon the
use of one's outstanding characteristic. The Laboratory sees
nothing inconsistent in declaring that accountants, auditors,
controllers, and bankers, cluster persistently enough in the bottom half of the structural scale to indicate the aptitude a handicap in these professions, and yet in the next breath asserting
that one whose experience, knowledge, skill, and opportunities, lie within these fields regard a high score, not as a burden,
but as indicating a valuable asset to be used constructively.

4

A renowned magazine editor, a prominent citizen of the United
States, excels nine men out of ten in structural visualization, and
UNUSED   yet, presumably ignoring this endowment, has
APTITUDES   made not only a rare place for himself in current affairs but without question a name for the
future. Can a test administrator or report writer tell such a
man of the world that he might be still greater? Perhaps in

abstract theory, but not in practice without awkward embarrassment. Yet unless one conceives humanity at its apex, the great individual must climb still higher; and with two world wars within the memory of a single generation, an ideal state seems still far distant. When an eminent man of today shows unmistakably an idle aptitude at least one interpretation is that he might have been still greater and so carried the twentieth-century world with him to new heights.

He may of course be regarded as disproving the apparent rule. But with the normal human being success checks with the intensive use of total ability; failure goes hand in hand with its partial application. While it sounds presumptuous to inform a prominent individual that he might have been still more distinguished, exactly this conclusion follows from carefully controlled research.

Occasionally one who excels in structural visualization trusts he uses the trait by his manner of cerebration, in building his plans, in analyzing his problems. Lawyers organize their cases and yet when actually measured score low. Most executives plan for the future and yet score low. Bankers, accountants, lawyers, writers, and executives in general, average low enough to suggest that such occupations do not force the use of this trait. Admitting that an exceptional individual in these fields may apply the gift, the statistical chances are that such a person is merely setting his goal too low to avoid the mental effort of raising his vocational standards.

5

Several independent reasoning processes lead to the conclusion that for increased assurance of success each person should
MANY APTITUDES use to the full every aptitude he possesses. A boy may not relish the idea of banking as a life's work, but cannot escape the fact that in this direction, and in closely allied regions, high accounting aptitude represents a valuable asset. Here only 3 per cent of those who survive grade D, only 3 per cent grade C (see the distribution curve for experienced accountants given in UNSOLVED BUSINESS PROBLEMS); while 80 per cent grade A. In this direction

FIGURE 5

Fields Suggested for Various Combinations of Aptitudes

		OBJECTIVITY		OTHER BROCHURES
HIGH STRUCTURAL VISUALIZATION				
HIGH ACCOUNTING APTITUDE	HIGH CREATIVE IMAGINATION	HIGH INDUCTIVE REASONING	ARCHITECTURE, COMMUNITY HOUSING, CONSULTING ENGINEERING	TOO-MANY-APTITUDE WOMAN
	LOW CREATIVE IMAGINATION	HIGH INDUCTIVE REASONING	ASTRONOMY (MATHEMATICAL), ASTROPHYSICS	INDIVIDUAL APPROACH TO SCIENTIFIC PROBLEMS
		LOW INDUCTIVE REASONING	CONTRACTING, COST ACCOUNTING, ESTIMATING, QUANTITY SURVEYS	UNSOLVED BUSINESS PROBLEMS
LOW ACCOUNTING APTITUDE	HIGH CREATIVE IMAGINATION	HIGH INDUCTIVE REASONING	SAFETY ENGINEERING	
		LOW INDUCTIVE REASONING	AIRPLANE DESIGN, ARCHITECTURAL SCULPTURE, AUTOMOBILE DESIGN, DESIGNING ENGINEERING, HEATING AND VENTILATING ENGINEERING, INVENTING, MUSICAL INSTRUMENT DESIGN	CHARACTERISTICS COMMON TO TECHNICAL ENGINEERS
	LOW CREATIVE IMAGINATION	HIGH INDUCTIVE REASONING	ARCHAEOLOGY, CRYSTALLOGRAPHY, GEOLOGY	INDIVIDUAL APPROACH TO SCIENTIFIC PROBLEMS
		LOW INDUCTIVE REASONING	AGRICULTURE, APPARATUS CONSTRUCTION, BIOLOGY, BUILDING CONSTRUCTION, CARPENTRY, CONSTRUCTION ENGINEERING, DIEMAKING, PLUMBING, TOOLMAKING	

FIGURE 5 (CONTINUED)

				OTHER BROCHURES
HIGH ACCOUNTING APTITUDE	LOW CREATIVE IMAGINATION	EXTREMELY SUBJECTIVE PERSONALITY	PERSONAL SECRETARIAL WORK	UNSOLVED BUSINESS PROBLEMS
		HIGH FINGER DEXTERITY	ADDING MACHINE OPERATION, BANKING (TELLER), STENOGRAPHY, TYPING	UNSOLVED BUSINESS PROBLEMS
		HIGH INDUCTIVE REASONING	ACTUARIAL WORK, BUSINESS RESEARCH, CORPORATION LAW, ECONOMICS, POPULATION STUDIES	UNSOLVED BUSINESS PROBLEMS
		OBJECTIVE PERSONALITY	BANKING EXECUTIVE WORK, EXECUTIVE SECRETARIAL WORK, INSURANCE	UNSOLVED BUSINESS PROBLEMS
		HIGH ANALYTICAL REASONING	ACCOUNTING	UNSOLVED BUSINESS PROBLEMS
		LOW ANALYTICAL REASONING	BOOKKEEPING, CLERICAL WORK	UNSOLVED BUSINESS PROBLEMS
LOW ACCOUNTING APTITUDE	HIGH CREATIVE IMAGINATION	HIGH INDUCTIVE REASONING	ART TEACHING, COLLEGE TEACHING, MINISTRY, NEWSPAPER REPORTING	OBJECTIVE APPROACH TO GROUP-INFLUENCING FIELDS
		LOW INDUCTIVE REASONING	TYPOGRAPHY	TOO-MANY-APTITUDE WOMAN
	LOW CREATIVE IMAGINATION	HIGH INDUCTIVE REASONING	ART CRITICISM, DEBATING, ESSAY WRITING	

LOW STRUCTURAL VISUALIZATION

boys who grade C or D in accounting aptitude have only an insignificant chance of success, only one twenty-seventh (3/80) the chance of the boy who grades A. Unless this last boy enters some region which demands the trait to the same extent as accounting, he wastes this gift, competing on equal footing with all of his contemporaries. This actually happens in teaching where 22 per cent of those who continue four years or more grade D in accounting aptitude, compared with 27 per cent who grade A. Here the boy high in accounting aptitude, grade A, striving for a place in the world, has little better chance of survival than one who grades D. Expressed in other words the boy who enters teaching might almost equally well grade D as A. One can argue that the characteristic must help in every field, that in teaching it makes easier the reading of themes, the marking of papers, the grading of examinations. But were this true then teachers high in accounting aptitude should continue more often than those low. The Laboratory believes no mortal certain enough of envisaged success to ignore lightly a tangible asset capable of multiplying twenty-seven times one's chance of realization.

Of teachers who survive four years or longer 15 per cent grade D in creative imagination as compared with 35 per cent who grade A. The latter have two and a third times (35/15) the chance of success possessed by the former. Again, where success depends on competition, it seems unwise to neglect creative imagination. But the same trait gives one no advantage in accounting, is perhaps a slight handicap. One who grades high in two traits, accounting aptitude and creative imagination, who happens to enter a field in which he uses the first no more than in teaching and the second no more than in accounting, might equally well grade D in both. Could the same person find work in which his chances of success because of his accounting aptitude are as good as in accounting and in which simultaneously his chances of success because of his creative imagination are as good as in teaching, work in which he uses both traits, his chances of success would be 27x2.3 or sixty-two times that of one who grades D in both.

Without as yet comparable figures for all directions, the Laboratory summarizes this in the phrase: one should use every aptitude one possesses. Probably no established occupation or profession inevitably and automatically demands any one combination; but some offer a more natural outlet than others for specific patterns, and this the Laboratory attempts to suggest schematically in figure 5. Of the thirteen aptitudes now measurable, almost every boy shows two, three, four, or more. Assuming that each exerted constructively in its proper direction improves his chances of success, could he turn all toward a mapped course, where each contributes, his tabulated chances of achieving a gratifying place for himself approach a certainty.

6

The rare adult who grades $A+$ in structural visualization pictures solid forms more quickly and surely than 95 per cent of other men. In many large organizations such

STRUCTURAL
VISUALIZATION
GRADE A PLUS

an individual puts new ideas into effect only so rapidly as he gains the approval of superiors of whom theoretically only one in twenty equals him in the trait; and instead of slowing his own mental caprices, especially when presenting a novel notion, he rebels at the deliberate pace of the group as a whole, the exasperating red tape, the irritating delays; and he soon autocratically states the correct answer with no attempt to explain it, refusing to review ploddingly his reasoning and so aid others to follow it. He may even reach his conclusions so rapidly and intuitively as to be unable to retrace the intricate steps. In consequence he withdraws into a disagreeable superciliousness, passively watching others struggle toward the answer he already visions. He trains subordinates, obviously duller than himself, who, because their speed more nearly parallels that of others, gain acceptance for his ideas and ultimate advancement for themselves; while he ends, despite his own measured superiority, at the foot of the group.

This lavishly-gifted man often achieves ampler compensation by working for himself, by developing a personal enterprise, with curbing responsibilities to no one, where only his own inability holds him back, where he competes with inexorable facts rather than with placable men.

7

Picking a life's work embraces two major considerations: the ultimate goal to which a boy aspires; and the road he takes in arriving. Stress of circumstances, unexpected emergencies, and procrastination, the postponement of facing the future until the last possible moment, too frequently drive him to heed exclusively the last, to enter the Human Engineering Laboratory expecting to try a number of sample jobs and learn categorically which actual position to seek or accept. This implies, whether intended or not, desire for a stationary niche; and few have this in mind. Instead at heart the ambitious boy wants somewhere to start, with the chance of promotion to wider responsibilities. But assured advancement does not take shape by chance, nor result alone from doing one's own job well, but is the foreseen outcome of thoughtful planning.

THE FUTURE

Many years ago the Laboratory picked, with extreme care, from a score of unemployed men one high in structural visualization and low in accounting aptitude to sweep the floor of a machine shop. Within a few weeks, in the absence of the regular operator, the mechanical superintendent gave the new floor man a chance to try his unskilled hand at the grinding wheel, the initial step toward his ultimately becoming a full-fledged machinist. Even when some months later the superintendent requisitioned another man like the first to replace his incipient craftsman, had the Laboratory said: 'We are sending you a born mechanic', he would have insisted he wanted no such person. Yet for nearly a decade he hired only unskilled sweepers, gradually developing them into a loyal group, familiar with every intricate machine, ready to overcome every technical obstacle.

Another man with identical aptitudes, high structural visualization and low accounting aptitude, put to cleaning a bank floor and granted a corresponding chance to show his worth at counting money or totaling a column of figures, commits such egregious errors that with everyone's consent he returns to his sweeping to remain there permanently. No matter how menial one's position, advancement depends upon aptitudes for the next job above, or for some emergency task, as much as upon recognized accomplishments. With this in mind the test administrator and report writer think so instinctively of the remote future that the forthcoming suggestions frequently seem bizarre.

Eight years ago, with a high-school sophomore, high in structural visualization and high in inductive reasoning, the test administrator mentioned diagnostic medicine as one of many activities believed to embrace these traits. The boy's ambition, it transpired, was medicine, fanned by an uncle in the profession who hoped his nephew might follow his footsteps. But repeated scholastic failure precluded all thought of college and a professional career. The illustration of diagnostic medicine reawoke the dormant question, to which we could only repeat that in aptitudes the boy scored as do many diagnosticians. The boy's former headmaster recently told us that he is now making a noteworthy place in second-year medical school, an accomplishment which, from the boy's scholastic record at the time of his test, appeared hopeless.

The child believes everything possible; only the academician admonishes that to reach professional medicine one must graduate from high school, enter college, rank high, graduate again, enter medical school, and graduate still again, only then to undertake an internship, hurdles which to the teacher appear insurmountable barriers for the poor student. Still further to the child the word medicine does not always connote the established profession in the mind of the reactionary, for numerous men, without medical degrees, play leading roles in public health, in the welfare of the nation.

In the course of a few years a trained test administrator sees individually several thousand boys and girls. He recognizes the apparent handicaps but steels himself to ignore those which cannot be measured; for he knows by years of experience that a boy who uses his aptitudes surprisingly often accomplishes the seemingly impossible. The Laboratory's philosophy of urging a goal ostensibly incapable of attainment rests on the belief that a man headed in what for want of a fitter term one may call the RIGHT direction advances from job to job as he grows older, further than he expected, further than anyone anticipated. To avoid turning him unwittingly into a blind alley, where he may reach a point at which he lacks the aptitudes for the next natural step, with no future toward which to strive, the Laboratory believes in aiming high, in thinking of top positions, of major occupations and professions.

8

In locating his own illusive path, each boy should set out by using his aptitudes in the order of their percentile scores; for, RELATIVE though illogical and unexpected, the relative preSCORES eminence of one's own aptitudes among themselves seems more significant both to worldly success and to satisfaction from work than excellence relative to others. While a high score in accounting aptitude, in comparison with other people, contributes to school success, or a low score to classroom failure, the degree by which the trait exceeds or falls below one's own structural visualization checks even more closely with academic accomplishments; so that a boy low in accounting aptitude, compared with others, but lower still in structural visualization, may sense no clerical hardships; while another, clearly high, but higher still in structural visualization, often exhibits paper-and-pencil shortcomings.

In practice the accuracies of aptitude tests seldom warrant such fine distinctions, but in theory a boy who grades A, or perhaps $A+$, in creative imagination, A in inductive reasoning, and lower, $A-$, in structural visualization, should consider teaching, which uses the first two, before such structural subjects as engineering and surgery. Another, who grades no higher in structure but lower in the other aptitudes, should consider first the structural fields.

A successful journalist scores at the seventy-eighth percentile in structural visualization, above three quarters of the adult male population, high enough to employ the gift satisfactorily in engineering, surgery, or architecture, and ordinarily to fidget, even to fail, in a non-structural field. But he scores still higher in three other traits, at the ninety-ninth percentile in creative imagination, at the ninety-eighth in inductive reasoning, at the ninety-second in analytical reasoning, all of which he applies successfully, for he writes special articles for a New York daily paper and enjoys the work. At the conclusion of his appointment he received an earlier edition of the present brochure which stresses structure; but how much the Laboratory should urge him to use it no one knows. Certainly the normal examinee should not force its use until he already uses the traits in which he scores higher.

Ideally the Laboratory should present each examinee with a brochure which discusses his aptitudes in the order of their percentile scores, manifestly impossible for this means eight thousand different texts. Consequently the test administrator picks the one which fits most closely. An examinee whose personal report contains only a list of scores without comment often feels slighted, but that is the kind of report toward which the Laboratory is working for in that case the brochure fits unquestionably; and obviously more thought goes into a brochure than into any one report. Only where a brochure falls short does the report writer attempt to interpret.

Occasionally an examinee's pattern of aptitudes falls between two of the Laboratory's present brochures. In this instance the test administrator gives one at the close of the appointment and, because the organization cannot afford to give two, asks the examinee to buy the second sometime in the future when he has digested the first.

The present brochure most often leaves in doubt one who grades B in structural visualization. The latest results suggest that, were the test perfectly accurate, all boys who grade A or B possess and should use the trait to the same extent, while those who grade C or D lack it. This means that every boy who grades B should use the trait to the same extent as one who grades A and with this in mind the Laboratory often seems to over-urge the use of structural visualization.

On the other hand, the accuracy of the structural tests is so low that one who actually grades B may not in reality possess the trait. To meet this defect, administrators give several trials, and in consequence the large percentage of battery time which goes toward the measurement of structural visualization calls undue attention to the trait by an enforced process which should in fact leave one skeptical of the outcome.

TABLE II

RELATIVE ACCURACIES OF 21 TESTS

TRAIT MEASURED	WORKSAMPLE NUMBER	ACCURACY OR RELIABILITY	AVERAGE CORRELATION WITH OTHER TESTS
Grip	185	0.96	0.07
Accounting Aptitude	268	0.93	0.11
Tonal Memory	77	0.90	0.08
Personality	35	0.89	0.06
Tapping	221	0.84	0.05
Pitch Discrimination	76	0.83	0.13
Tweezer Dexterity	18	0.82	0.11
Number Memory	165	0.82	0.16
Creative Imagination	161	0.80	0.12
Accounting Aptitude	1	0.78	0.14
Finger Dexterity	16	0.78	0.16
Inductive Reasoning	164F	0.77	0.16
Clock Reversal (Experimental)	170	0.76	0.09
Structural Visualization	167	0.73	0.15
Observation	206	0.69	0.18
Inductive Reasoning	164C	0.67	0.11
Structural Visualization	204	0.67	0.18
Analytical Reasoning	244	0.66	0.25
Memory for Design	294	0.66	0.24
Length Discrimination	264	0.49	0.12
Structural Visualization	5	0.40	0.20

THE HUMAN ENGINEERING LABORATORY AIMS TO MEASURE SEPARATE TRAITS WITH PERFECT RELIABILITY (1.00), THIRD COLUMN, AND AT THE SAME TIME INDEPENDENTLY OF OTHER TRAITS (CORRELATION 0.00), LAST COLUMN TO THE RIGHT. ACCURACIES OR RELIABILITIES OF 0.90 OR ABOVE IT CONSIDERS EXCELLENT, THOSE ABOVE 0.80 AS SATISFACTORY, THOSE ABOVE 0.70 AS USABLE, AND THOSE BELOW THIS AS CHALLENGING FURTHER RESEARCH. INTERCORRELATIONS WITH TESTS OF OTHER TRAITS LESS THAN 0.10 IT REGARDS AS SHOWING SATISFACTORY INDEPENDENCE, THOSE OF 0.20 AND ABOVE AS UNSATISFACTORY. WITH IMPROVED ACCURACY OF MEASUREMENT, AT THE TOP, COMES INCREASED INDEPENDENCE.

9

A trained statistician expresses accuracy, or in technical language RELIABILITY, by the mathematical agreement or disagreement among several measurements of the same

ACCURACY OR
RELIABILITY

quantity. An inquisitive boy does much the same when, on weighing himself twice and getting different answers, he promptly condemns the scale as out of order. Perhaps sensing that he may have misread the figures, he steps on the platform again to check. A slight variation he accepts as near enough; but the greater the inconsistency the more he doubts.

Perfect agreement among results, or with aptitude measurements agreement among several trials of a test, statisticians call an accuracy or reliability of unity (1.00); complete disagreement, so that one trial gives no indication of another, they call a reliability of zero (0.00).

The reliability of the word-association test, worksample 35, form AE, a measure of personality discussed in section v, approaches unity, 0.92, one of the highest accuracies obtained by the research department in evaluating an aptitude. The raising of this from 0.73, at which it began, to the present figure has required constant research for twenty years and in consequence the reliability of form DE, on which the staff has worked no more than five years, is less (0.76). The reliability of the number-checking test, worksample 1, is 0.78-0.87, as shown in table II which lists the present minimum reliabilities and average intercorrelations of twenty-one aptitude tests.

10

A single trial of the wiggly block means little. The average of two, taken under controlled conditions, is slightly more indica-

INACCURACY
OF STRUCTURAL
VISUALIZATION TESTS

tive, with an average reliability of 0.50, and a minimum reliability which may be as low as 0.40, the value used in table II. The average reliability of three trials is approximately 0.55, of four 0.60, although the exact mathematical figure is extremely doubtful, because to save time the

FIGURE 6

RELATION BETWEEN TWO MEASURES OF STRUCTURAL VISUALIZATION

BLACK-CUBE GRADES, WORKSAMPLES 167 AND 204

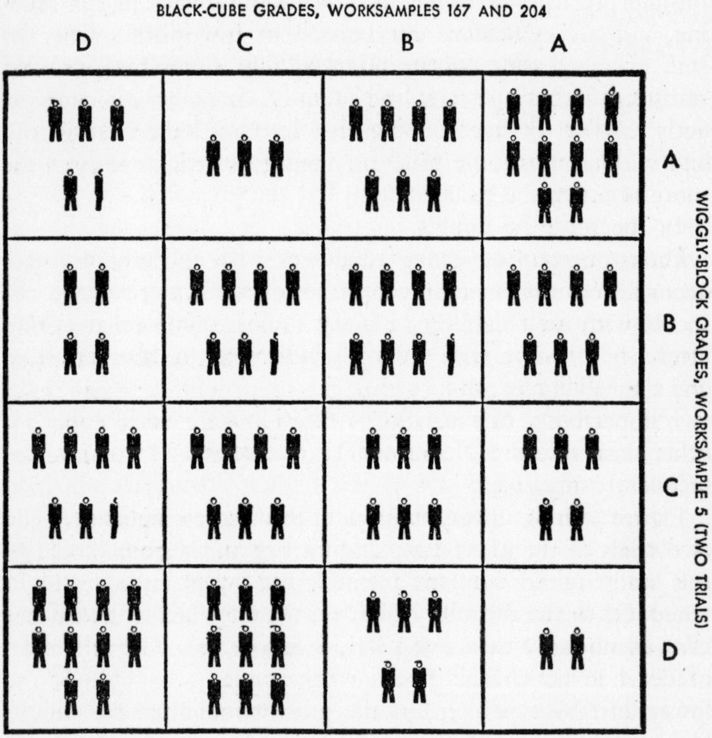

THIS FIGURE SHOWS HOW INACCURATE ARE THE LABORATORY'S MEASUREMENTS OF STRUCTURAL VISUALIZATION. OF 585 MEN, AGES 19 AND OVER, 2 IN EVERY HUNDRED (2 PER CENT) GRADE D IN THE WIGGLY BLOCK (AVERAGE OF TWO TRIALS) AND A IN THE BLACK CUBE (LOWER RIGHT). FIVE IN EVERY HUNDRED (UPPER LEFT) GRADE A IN THE WIGGLY BLOCK AND D IN THE BLACK CUBE, THE MATHEMATICAL CORRELATION EQUALING ONLY 0.32. TO GAIN ACCURACY THE LABORATORY AVERAGES THE TWO WORKSAMPLES AND GIVES THREE OR FOUR TRIALS OF THE WIGGLY BLOCK, WEIGHTING IT TWICE BECAUSE OF ITS GREATER SIGNIFICANCE.

Laboratory rarely gives four trials to those who are clearly low. In the course of its research the staff at one time thought a long first trial corrupted either by nervousness or by a failure to understand instructions, but finds no statistical evidence to corroborate the assumption. At another it unsuccessfully attempted to prove an exceptionally poor trial uncertain enough to neglect. Because a disturbing factor of almost any sort lowers a priori a test score, because nervousness probably leads to an unduly long time together with errors, because a misinterpretation of instructions no doubt delays one in starting, and any extraneous interruption lengthens one's time, the staff averaged the best three out of four trials; but again no statistical analysis justifies the practice. Long trials occur exactly as often as expected from the laws of chance. Ordinarily and within limits the greater the number of trials averaged the more accurate the result.

In the readings from a single scale any discrepancy shows without question a mistake somewhere; but the reverse, exact accord, does not invariably prove accuracy. A scale may coincide with itself perfectly and yet disagree with others. Only after a boy has weighed himself several times on several scales, and they all agree, can he accept the result with certainty. Like two imperfect scales, the wiggly block and the black cube, another instrument for approximating structural visualization, frequently disagree.

Figure 6 shows diagrammatically the disagreements between two trials of the black cube and two of the wiggly block. In this study results for two forms of the black cube are combined. Of the total group of 585 men, age 19 and over, ten per cent, symbolized by the ten figures in the upper right corner, grade A in both tests. Ten per cent grade D in both at the lower left. Nine per cent grade D in two trials of the wiggly block, worksample 5, but C in the black cube, worksamples 167 or 204, shown in the second square from the left in the lowest row. Five per cent grade D in the wiggly block and B in the black cube; while two per cent grade D in the wiggly block and A in the black cube, shown in the lower right.

For 422 males, ages 20 and up, the correlation between the wiggly-block final score, the average usually of three or four trials, and a single trial of the black cube, worksample 204, is 0.55; while with the average of two trials of the black cube it improves to 0.64. With these considerations in mind one must face a possible, almost a probable, inaccuracy in one's structural-visualization result, but accept it as an approximation.

To avoid the feeling of uncertainty always aroused by obvious conflicts, the scoring department might send merely the computed final average, the most accurate indication of the underlying aptitude. But many examinees appreciate a detailed record, for they remember a particularly fast and lucky trial or another for some odd reason extraordinarily long; and the Laboratory repeats trials to stumble on just such discrepancies and average them out; for the average of widely dissimilar scores is exactly as accurate as the average of as many identical ones. The accuracy of a test is shown by its statistical reliability, not by the chance coincidence of scores for one person.

For illustration, postulate a worthless test, of no statistical value, with a reliability of zero (0.00), in which an examinee grades A or D by luck. Of four examinees, with two trials each, one grades A on first trial and A on second; one grades A on first and D on second; a third grades D on first and A on second; a fourth D on first and D on second. Such disparity as A on first trial with D on second occurs exactly as often as one expects on the assumption of pure chance, of zero reliability; and conversely agreement of trials, A on first followed by A on second, is no more significant despite one's impression.

With the wiggly block, agreement between the first and second trials occurs exactly as often as one expects with the known reliability. The average of trials which disagree, and so make one distrust the result, is exactly as accurate as the average of trials which agree, the accuracy or inaccuracy of the average depending upon the accuracy or reliability of the measuring instrument. As the Laboratory's norms are based on the average of all trials, regardless of discrepancies, each individual must average all of his trials before comparing himself with others.

A seriously minded boy, from a family of engineers and brought up with the tacit assurance of following his father's calling, scored low on the first trial of the wiggly block, perhaps, the administrator thought, through failure to understand the task and so want of confidence in approaching it. On second trial the boy improved markedly, and on third graded A. On fourth trial he dropped back, perchance through boredom.

Mathematically the boy averaged C, but in the considered opinion of a trained administrator warranted a higher mark. The report gave the computed average but also explained the administrator's feeling and suggested that because of the father's position in engineering and the boy's opportunity in that direction, the boy try chemistry and if successful physics, both required by most engineering schools, advice not ordinarily given a boy grading C. The boy failed both subjects and in consequence spent an extra year in high school.

In a second test appointment, several years later, the boy graded D in two additional structural-visualization tests and without doubt is low in this aptitude. Despite the Laboratory's endeavor to measure accurately and impersonally, opinions enter inadvertently more than one intends. Here the situation misled the test administrator, the father, and the boy himself, all with the best of intentions. To gain the advantage of aptitude tests and avoid the waste of just such rationalization one must score results objectively, mathematically.

II

Assembly times for the eight-piece pyramid, worksample 68, now sometimes administered with an introductory one of four

THE PYRAMID   pieces and called worksamples 231 and 232, check even more closely with engineering-school marks and survival. Partly because this test fits most satisfactorily in the third appointment and yet should be taken before a boy makes his final decision to enter an engineering school, the Laboratory recommends a first appointment at age 9 or 10 including a first structural test and so an approximation of structural visualization, a second appointment about two years later involving a second structural test, and finally a third appointment including the pyramid, before a boy decides on an engineering or technical school and so starts probably for some part of the immense field of engineering.

Approximately half of the adult men who try the pyramid fail to assemble it, or to approach a solution, in the fifteen or twenty minutes of battery time ordinarily allowed. As yet the research department lacks comparable figures for women.

12

An occasional school executive, to assay the predictive accuracy of aptitude tests, still requests the Laboratory to measure

SIX MONTHS SAVED

a pupil intimately known to the faculty and then declares inaccurate results which fail in any respect to paint the accepted picture. Every conscientious headmaster recognizes his own inability to predict each boy's relative chances in various courses. He remembers some who tried college against his own best advice and succeeded; others, with every prospect of academic success, who for some inexplicable reason failed. Anyone who acknowledges such doubts, after a full year's association or more, must realize the corresponding uncertainties of the Laboratory's report based upon a few hours. On the other hand, the most hesitant headmaster gives intelligently considered counsel, which usually proves correct even though occasionally wrong.

An industrialist recently summarized a dozen years' experience in the application of aptitude-test results by saying that a Human Engineering Laboratory report now gives him as clear an understanding of each new employee as he formerly possessed at the end of the first six months. Assuming the Laboratory's results no more accurate than one man's opinion of another at the end of the first half year, this adjustment period in a new position is financially expensive. In the business world it means high labor turnover and frequent accidents while the foreman tries the new man at unfamiliar work. In their initial six months salesmen return little or nothing but must be paid enough to carry them. More serious than any of these the new employee does poor work, which if caught by an inspector means waste of materials and of previous work done by skilled employees on the same piece spoiled later by the new man, and if allowed to pass as nearly perfect causes complaints from customers. Accidents happen even after the first six months but not so often, labor turnover continues but not to the same extent, mistakes occur but less frequently; for this period indicates a tentative course, shows how to correct the new employee's mistakes, gives some idea of the departments where he fits easily or where he proves entirely out of place.

On the basis of Human Engineering Laboratory test scores, this industrial executive now starts each new employee with as clear-cut an understanding of where he belongs as he formerly had at the end of the first half year, maps a program at the beginning which he finds, from experience, about as indicative as the one formerly reached after six months. Thus he saves himself, his organization, and the new worker, a disconcerting period of adjustment and uncertainty.

If a business executive, who carries a man on his payroll five, ten, or more years, values six months gained at the outset, the preparatory-school teacher, with a boy in his care no more than three or four years, should appreciate still more a similar saving at the beginning for here six months represents a significant fraction of the total time. He should use worksample results as do business executives, as a basis on which to plan a tentative program for each new boy, to be followed carefully and revised when necessary, but one which will prove as satisfactory from the start as one arrived at several months later without test scores.

At the time of the test appointment, the Laboratory asks each boy's permission to send a copy of his report to his school principal, headmaster, dean, or teacher. It suggests that a boy forward his scores directly to any new school he hopes to enter and include a copy with his college admission papers.

As the Laboratory tests some ten thousand persons annually, a school or college executive may find that a substantial percentage of his new boys have already been measured. With the boy's permission he can always obtain copies of reports directly from the Laboratory. See information pamphlet.

13

Why does one do well at such a task as assembling the wiggly block, the black cube, or the pyramid? It is not pure luck. Is

PRACTICE it previous experience; or is one inherently capable? On answers to just such questions depend both the abstract theory and the practical application of aptitude testing. The rhetorical question: ' But can I not train any boy to score high? ', advanced by skeptics as argument against aptitude tests, is indubitably true. Everyone learns by repetition. No matter how low a test score a boy may succeed in that direction. One who wishes above all else to paint, to play the piano, or to build bridges, may do so regardless of obstacles providing he expends sufficient effort, for in life an appallingly handicapped man or woman by sheer hard work often far outstrips gifted companions. For confirmation turn to figure 16, page 81, which shows that of 43 college men only one who graded D in accounting aptitude graduated with a bachelor-of-arts degree. But this exception received honors.

With the wiggly block, worksample 5, a statistically-normal examinee who completes the first trial in 3.00 minutes consumes only 1.88 minutes on second trial, 1.57 minutes on third, and only 1.50 on fourth. Expressed in other terms a second trial of the wiggly block betters the first by 38 per cent, a third betters the first by 48 per cent, and a fourth by 50 per cent. Research findings annually reconfirm the statement that anyone acquires skill.

Even when disturbed on one trial by some extraneous factor called hard luck, an examinee who takes longer than standard improves as expected on the next trial. Dotting at top speed with a pencil, or with a corresponding stylus on worksample 221, the tapping test, where fatigue accumulates more rapidly than practice, an examinee goes slower in each consecutive three-second period, so that superficially he gradually retrogresses. But after a half minute complete rest the fatigue disappears and he taps more than ever in the next three seconds, for the effect of practice remains. On every repetition of every task a boy gains a facility which enables him to perform thereafter more rapidly or more accurately.

This holds equally and to identically the same quantitative extent for the boy who does poorly on the initial trial, grade D, and for the one who does well, grade A. Improvement with practice is constant for all persons when expressed as a ratio of second trial to first; the boy who ranks low improves the same proportion as one who ranks high.

In line with this finding the Laboratory applies to each trial of each test, an empirically determined practice factor. Individual performances vary widely, but in general the second-trial time on the wiggly block, worksample 5, multiplied by 1.60 reproduces the corresponding first-trial time. Expressed symbolically:

$$\text{I} \qquad \frac{\text{first trial time}}{\text{second trial time}} = 1.60 \text{ (practice factor for second trial).}$$

This applies to all percentiles on the scoring scale, so that:

$$\text{II} \qquad \frac{\text{90th percentile 1st trial time}}{\text{90th percentile 2nd trial time}} = \frac{\text{50th percentile 1st trial time}}{\text{50th percentile 2nd trial time}};$$

or one might substitute any percentile in place of the ninetieth and of the fiftieth.

With each additional trial the effect of practice lessens, the practice factor for the third consecutive trial of worksample 5 equaling 1.91, and for the fourth 2.00. The time for the second trial is 62 per cent that of the first, the reciprocal of the practice factor, 1.60, that is, the second trial is 38 per cent shorter than the first. The third trial is only 16 per cent shorter than the second, and the fourth only 5 per cent shorter than the third.

Were excellence in the wiggly block due to previous practice, to playing with blocks as a child, then boys who grade A when tested must be regarded as already partly experienced. If such early training with blocks be equivalent to two standard trials, enough to raise a boy's letter grade from D to C or from C to B, but not enough to raise his grade from D to A, then his first apparent Laboratory trial represents in reality his third actual trial. Under these conditions, improvement on repetition should equal that normally found between third and fourth trials, or about 5 per cent, significantly less than the 38-per-cent improvement between first and second trials. As a corollary, were low scores in the test due to lack of previous experience, to not having played with blocks as a child, then boys who grade below average should with practice improve more than normal. The surprising discovery that improvement with practice is constant for those who grade A and those who grade D offers strong evidence that excellence in the wiggly block is not due to previous practice.

14

Performance improves with age as well as with practice until curves reach an adult plateau at seventeen or eighteen beyond AGE FACTORS which age exerts no further effect. Were improvement with age the result of intervening practice, of accumulating experience, were it acquired skill, then in light of the Laboratory's study of practice the group of boys who grade *A*, when young, should reach the plateau sooner and should probably improve less as they grow older than the group who grade low. But when improvement is computed as with practice, by dividing the score at the adult plateau into the corresponding score for any other age, the ratio is the same for those who grade high and low.

Any distribution curve, figure 17, multiplied by a constant gives the corresponding distribution for another age. The ratio of the fiftieth percentile for one age to the fiftieth percentile for another equals the ratio of the ninetieth percentiles for the same ages:

$$\text{III} \quad \frac{90\text{th percentile (adult)}}{90\text{th percentile (age 14)}} = \frac{50\text{th percentile (adult)}}{50\text{th percentile (age 14)}} = \text{age factor (age 14)}.$$

The constant by which one multiplies the curve for one age to obtain the corresponding curve for adults of the same sex the staff calls the AGE FACTOR. The constancy of the age factor, of improvement with age, suggests that change with age is not the result of further practice and additional experience.

15

Such evidence as that just presented coincides with the premise that structural visualization is inherited. This possibility exceeds anything which can be proved, and INHERITANCE OF yet may form the nucleus of an integrated STRUCTURAL experimental program. For science gradu- VISUALIZATION ally restricts the ultimate truth to ever narrowing bounds by disproving innumerable theories, never confirming one directly and irrefutably. Tomorrow new facts, more exact measurements, altered conditions, reveal limitations or the complete failure of a law which previously fitted all known instances, and so drive one to a sounder working hypothesis. A theory is in effect a short-lived scaffolding doomed from the outset to almost inevitable disproof, erected to aid in the building of an experimental program, by means of which the experimenter advances. Once a measurement is made, recorded, and confirmed, which fails to fit he willingly scraps his scaffolding. With this in mind the genuine scientist utters his theory, not as a cherished conviction, but with clear precision, that he may apply it intelligently and so finally disprove it, thus limiting more narrowly the remaining region in which he thereafter seeks verity. The habitual practice, followed by inexperienced amateurs, of guarding their reputations with vague and circumspect conclusions which no one can either apply with certainty or disprove conclusively, contributes nothing to scientific advance. Were eternal truth obvious or recognizable when met, one should certainly reserve one's judgment; but unerring progress consists, not in opening the right door, but in closing and locking wrong ones until only a single passable way remains.

In the physical domain parents recognize and act on the nice distinction between inherited and acquired characteristics, even though biology's latest developments tend to blur the sharp distinction by showing that superficial appearances may be either. The practical world accepts blue eyes or brown, even bodily height, as predetermined, though chemicals and glandular action alter the latter slightly. With mental characteristics parents and teachers find it harder to know what to accept as fixed and where in consequence to expend energy toward effective change. Traits which evidence suggests are inherited the Laboratory terms APTITUDES and recommends that, awaiting further research, they be considered stable and energy toward change concentrated elsewhere even though biologists will no doubt someday find means of changing them much as they now influence physical appearances known to be inherited and once thought fast in consequence.

At 19 or just prior to this age, figure 7, boys attain the adult plateau in structural visualization, much as in physical height, and thereafter show no further measurable change. Girls reach

FIGURE 7

GROWTH OF STRUCTURAL VISUALIZATION
FOR MEN AND WOMEN

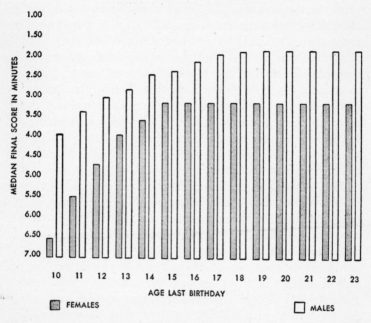

AGE LAST BIRTHDAY

▨ FEMALES   ☐ MALES

WITH MEN, WHITE VERTICAL BARS, STRUCTURAL VISUALIZATION AS MEASURED BY WORK-SAMPLES 4 AND 5 GROWS GRADUALLY FROM AGE 10 AT THE EXTREME LEFT TO AGE 19 WHERE IT REACHES MATURITY. WITH WOMEN, AS SHOWN BY THE DARK BARS, THE SAME TRAIT STARTS LOWER BUT GROWS MORE RAPIDLY, REACHING MATURITY AT 15, FOUR YEARS EARLIER THAN WITH BOYS. AT THIS POINT BOYS AND GIRLS ARE MORE ALIKE IN THIS MASCULINE TRAIT THAN EITHER BEFORE OR AFTER.

stable maturity three or four years earlier, at age 15. Engineering-school years fail to affect the trait. Technical experience exerts no influence, for brilliant engineers and scientists score no higher than the top nineteen-year-old boy. Students and teachers waste the energy they spend in trying to change this trait after age 19. Certainly from a practical standpoint, energy spent in other directions produces more significant results.

Pursuing to its logical conclusion the hypothesis that structural visualization is inherited, it must be sex linked, for adult men differ strikingly from adult women. Expressed in genetic terminology, the trait depends upon a gene of the X chromosome. Since, according to the laws of inheritance, this never passes from father to son, and since the Y, until proved effective, may in so hypothetical a discussion be ignored, structural visualization never descends from father to son, but instead from father to daughter, and thence to grandson. Pursuing this ephemeral chain of conjecture, males, with a single X chromosome each, should show a sex-linked trait in half the cases. Daughters, on the other hand, with two X chromosomes, one from the father, one from the mother, should exhibit structural visualization three-quarters of the time if dominant, one quarter if recessive. Since women average significantly below men and the trait in consequence appears less commonly in daughters than in fathers, it must be recessive rather than dominant.

The conclusion that a recessive structural visualization should appear with one quarter of females and one half of males can be tested experimentally, for it implies that in structural tests the seventy-fifth (75) percentile for women should equal the fiftieth (50) percentile for men. A tentative study of wiggly-block scores made by Barrows and Weston shows that in reality these two points correspond.

Originators of aptitude tests endeavor normally to spread the population over the scoring scale, discarding or revising tests found impossible or unduly troublesome by more than a few per cent. But if structural visualization prove sex linked, and certainly men excel women, the experimenter should investigate structural tests adjusted only to the fastest half of men and to the fastest quarter of women. Structural visualization, which on this assumption descends from father to daughter, never from father to son, may nevertheless appear in the son through the single X chromosome which he receives from the mother. Fathers with the trait should in one half the cases have sons who receive it from mothers who in turn may not show it because of its recessive nature. Fathers successful in manufacturing, engineering, surgery, or science, probably high in structural visualization, should realize their own sons may not inherit it. But fathers who lack the trait should equally often have sons who show it.

16

The specific decision of law versus engineering comes up surprisingly often, perhaps because structural visualization descends from mother to son. A father without the trait and successful in a non-structural pursuit, as law, regards his son's interest in machines, engines, and mechanical gimcracks as juvenile and likely to be outgrown. Yet as often as once a week a mature man, a law graduate, comes to the Laboratory after several years in his father's office unhappy with his progress. Too frequently he hopes to turn headlong in some new direction, toward engineering, manufacturing, or science, insisting that the test administrator answer specifically where he should go next.

LAW VERSUS ENGINEERING

Table III lists in parallel columns traits believed typical, at the left, of lawyers and, at the right, of designing engineers and engineering executives. The latter groups average high in structural visualization, the former, low. Should a boy give up

TABLE III

Comparison of Law and Engineering

TRAIT	LAW	DESIGNING ENGINEERING	ENGINEERING EXECUTIVE WORK
STRUCTURAL VISUALIZATION	LOW	HIGH	HIGH
INDUCTIVE REASONING	HIGH	—	—
CREATIVE IMAGINATION	—	HIGH	LOW
PERSONALITY	EXTREMELY SUBJECTIVE	SUBJECTIVE	OBJECTIVE

an assured future in his father's established firm, and turn to engineering, merely because of an intangible aptitude?

A host of important intellectual undertakings of the recent past lie halfway between two subjects once distinct enough to name separately. ELECTRO-CHEMISTRY implies the application of electrical techniques to the science of chemistry and demands on the part of one person an intimate knowledge of both subjects. ELECTRO-CARDIOGRAPHY combines electricity with a study of the heart; BIOCHEMISTRY designates the chemistry of living matter; ASTROPHYSICS is a combination of astronomy and physics; GEO-CHEMISTRY, a study of the chemical changes of the earth. Ancient departments of knowledge reveal by their names an origin between previously established subjects: GEOGRAPHY is a combination of the study of the earth with a study of drawing; GEOMETRY is a study of the earth combined with a study of measurement. Some boy ignoring neither his high structural visualization nor inspiring opportunities in law, by applying scientific methods to legal problems, might carry jurisprudence to unimagined heights.

17

The Human Engineering Laboratory developed from an attempt to apply engineering methods to an understanding of human beings. Largely for this reason the Laboratory recommends the exact sciences, physics, chemistry, mathematics, and astronomy, especially to one high in structural visualization who plans to join the Laboratory staff. One should know English, history, philosophy, and the fine arts, as well as economics, psychology, sociology, education, and government, all as a part of one's general background. But these last fields are as yet so inexact that the one right answer is seldom known. A boy may think in almost any way he sees fit and find authorities to support him. He may be right; but if clearly wrong a teacher finds it extremely difficult in these unformed fields to prove to him his error. Even the general direction of the future is not yet set. These subjects offer unlimited opportunities; but they are regions in which to experiment, to apply one's training, not to acquire it.

In the exact sciences a boy can more frequently be shown his specific error. In the solution of a mathematical problem one who adds incorrectly is clearly wrong at that point and his error found. Work in these so-called exact sciences gives a boy a chance to test his own embryonic thought processes among established rules. Reasoning processes which produce the right answer in known fields are less apt to go astray in uncharted regions.

TRAINING FOR HUMAN ENGINEERING

18

The hypothesis that each man's mental make-up breaks into mathematically distinct factors or aptitudes, each dependent on the presence or absence of some gene within a chromosome, will never be proved but serves as an admirable frame about which to plan experiments. It means that the Laboratory should be able to measure these factors separately and study each independent of the remainder. This simplifies the problem, for if one of these factors can be isolated it can be studied as a single discrete variable regardless of the tantalizing part it plays in the far more intricate ensemble.

BIMODAL
DISTRIBUTIONS

The baffling complexity of the human mind makes many regard as impossible its scientific study. But if one factor at a time can be separated from all others it becomes merely a matter of persistence to study them one by one.

If each trait is due to the presence or absence of a gene, the distribution curve for structural visualization should break at the critical point, at the fiftieth percentile for men and the seventy-fifth for women, displaying either a gap at this point between two modes or a mode above and a straggling out below. In exact accord with the theory of inheritance an examinee should possess the gene which causes structural visualization or lack it, should possess each trait in full or not at all, or more exactly some persons should possess one trait to the full, the dominant trait, and others lack this but possess instead the corresponding recessive trait.

In most tests a majority of persons score average and only a few exceptionally high or equally low. See, for instance, the distribution of accounting aptitude among boys, page 84.

The word-association test is the first indication that the Laboratory has not merely spread persons out on a scale but has actually divided them into two separate types. Figure 3, of UNSOLVED BUSINESS PROBLEMS, based on 1420 adult males, shows an unmistakable gap at the twenty-fifth percentile, between the extremely subjective quarter and the rest of the population. Figure 18, in THE TOO-MANY-APTITUDE WOMAN, suggests a similar gap in the word-association distribution curves for girls of three separate ages, less clearly defined but lying unmistakably between the twenty-fifth and fiftieth percentiles. Figure 8 of the present volume gives distribution curves for the same test for boys of three ages. Each shows a shallow region around the twenty-fifth percentile, between five and twelve significant responses.

The word-association test shows no sex difference. The trait which it measures, if inherited, is not sex linked. On this hypothesis three quarters of the population should possess the dominant component and one quarter the recessive. The actual gap divides the population into these proportions.

The present accuracy of the word-association test (0.89-0.93) is the result of fifteen years of constant research. When the test as first scored gave a reliability in the vicinity of 0.70, the distribution showed no recognizable bimodal tendency. Even when after ten years of additional study the reliability reached 0.85 the distribution still showed no gap. Only when the reliability bettered ninety did it finally appear. The accuracy of the structural-visualization tests is not as yet great enough (reliability 0.40-0.60) to show the gap even were it present. Not until the accuracy reaches 0.90, if that time ever arrives, can one expect the bimodal configuration.

Another objection to the inheritance theory is that too large a percentage of the traits thus far studied seem to be sex linked, at least three among the thirteen now measurable; whereas by the laws of pure chance perhaps less than one in twenty should show this feature. A conceivable explanation is that traits in which men and women differ come daily to one's attention, are more noticeable, more apt to be measured than others possessed by everyone and so taken for granted.

19

One school of philosophers believes that science is the organization of facts into an orderly pattern. Certainly science cannot continue indefinitely to amass data A NATURAL LAW but must arrange it to simplify its assimilation and to predict future phenomena. Any relation between two previously disconnected facts is a step in advance.

FIGURE 8

BIMODAL CURVES INDICATING COMPLEMENTARY TRAITS

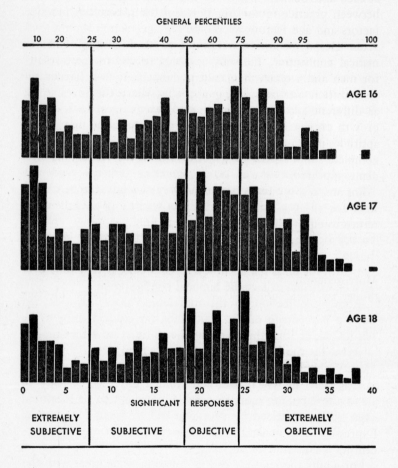

GENERAL PERCENTILES

BOYS GROUP BELOW AND ABOVE THE TWENTY-FIFTH PERCENTILE. COMPARATIVELY FEW SCORE
BETWEEN THE TWENTIETH AND THE FORTIETH, SUGGESTING TWO TYPES OF PERSONS:
THOSE WHO SCORE EXTREMELY SUBJECTIVE, BETWEEN 0 AND 7 SIGNIFICANT RESPONSES,
AND THE LARGER OBJECTIVE GROUP WHO SCORE BETWEEN 8 AND 40 ON THE BOTTOM
SCALE. BASED ON 379 BOYS AGE 16, 509 AGE 17, AND 369 AGE 18, THESE DISTRIBUTIONS
SHOW THE GAP AT THE TWENTY-FIFTH PERCENTILE, TOP SCALE, MORE CLEARLY THAN THE
CORRESPONDING CURVES FOR GIRLS BASED ON SMALLER POPULATIONS (SEE THE TOO-MANY-
APTITUDE WOMAN, PAGE 110), BUT NOT SO SHARPLY AS THE CURVE IN UNSOLVED BUSINESS
PROBLEMS, PAGE 14, BASED ON A STILL LARGER GROUP, 1420 ADULT MEN.

For many years the research department obtained separately for men and for women a purely empirical practice factor for each trial of each test and similarly an age factor for each sex at each age, but felt intuitively that some relation should exist between practice factors for different trials, between practice factors and age factors, even between age factors for the two sexes. Despite numerous attempts to find a simple mathematical connection, the staff has been forced to treat results for men and women independently especially with structural visualization and accounting aptitude where the sexes grow at different rates and mature at different ages, so that the growth curves are not parallel. As the number of measurable aptitudes increased this was becoming unwieldy when the most complete simplification which the Laboratory has found suddenly appeared. One can state it as follows:

For any one aptitude the ratio of any two percentiles is constant for all ages, all trials, and both sexes. For partial proof, return to equation III, page 32. Transposing:

$$\text{IV} \qquad \frac{\text{90th percentile (age 14)}}{\text{50th percentile (age 14)}} = \frac{\text{90th percentile (adult)}}{\text{50th percentile (adult)}}.$$

More generally this becomes: For any given aptitude the ratio of any two percentiles is constant for all ages. Samuel Horton of the research department has proved this to hold for four aptitudes: accounting aptitude, finger dexterity, tweezer dexterity, and creative imagination; and Florence Hauck has shown it to apply to structural visualization.

Transposing in like manner equation II:

$$\text{V} \qquad \frac{\text{90th percentile first trial}}{\text{50th percentile first trial}} = \frac{\text{90th percentile second trial}}{\text{50th percentile second trial}}.$$

Expressed more generally in words the ratio of any two percentiles is constant for all trials.

For adults the left side of this equation is identical with the right side of equation IV. Thus: For any one aptitude the ratio of any two percentiles is constant for all ages and all trials.

Empirically the ratio of any two percentiles for men equals the corresponding ratio for women, the final law becoming: For any one aptitude the ratio of any two percentiles is constant for all ages, all trials, and both sexes.

20

One, elusive qualification should be noted; the identical improvement with regular practice for those who score high and EDUCATION low depends upon the manner of computing improvement. With every complete repetition of a set task normal examinees in all parts of the scoring scale gain the same amount. But for every hour spent at the same task, grade-*A* boys improve more than grade-*D* and soon leave the latter far behind, for in a given length of time those who grade *A* repeat any appointed task several times, while the slower who grade *D* do it only once or never finish.

Recognition of this fact underlies the Laboratory's educational recommendations. Pupils who grade *D* in structural visualization should not work in the same classroom with pupils who grade *A*, for under such conditions the two cannot repeat a structural task an equal number of times. One who grades *D*, and must be stopped in the middle, grows hopelessly confused, while one who grades *A* becomes bored if forced to wait. One 16-year-old boy in every six finishes the six-piece wiggly block, worksample 4, in approximately one minute, another in every six takes four minutes or more. Where the pace is set for the latter, the other wastes three quarters of his time waiting. If the pace be set for the fast pupil, the slow one finishes only a quarter of each assignment and inevitably acquires the bewildered expression which so often appears on the faces of so-called poor students. Ordinarily an experienced teacher fits the educational pace to the average (median) boy. Judging by wiggly-block times, this means that the fast boy in every six wastes half his learning time; while the slow boy finishes only half of each assigned task.

Were there but a single unit aptitude, then a boy's only course would be unremitting labor to overcome the inherent lack, and the realization that, no matter how great his efforts, another more gifted might momentarily overtake and pass him with ease. But with thirteen distinct, known traits, a boy who scores lower than another in the wiggly block or in any aptitude, who needs many more trials to gain equal excellence, frequently scores clearly high elsewhere.

On the assumption of thirteen aptitudes, recognized in 1940 (see UNSOLVED BUSINESS PROBLEMS), nearly half of all boys possess either six or seven, no more and no less. Remarkably alike in the total quantity of ability the members of this entire group should arrive at their ultimate goals in the same length of time, those slow at certain tasks advancing correspondingly fast at others. Pupils who grade D in structural visualization should go slow in subjects requiring it, regaining this lost time in subjects demanding aptitudes in which they grade A.

There are today enough schools, and enough classes within each, so that a practical step toward this ideal solution is to guide those who grade D in structural visualization toward one school, those who grade A toward another. Table VIII, at the end of this brochure, lists technical and engineering schools which the Laboratory suggests to boys who grade A (men's norms) in structural visualization. Here the boy with this trait may progress at maximum speed in structural subjects. Table IX, page 142, lists general colleges and universities offering degrees in engineering, which the Laboratory recommends to grade B structural visualization. Finally, table X gathers together non-engineering, non-technical men's colleges, which the Laboratory recommends to those who grade C and D in structural visualization. Here the boy low in structure finds a group who travel rapidly in other directions.

21

A penchant for languages probably exists, for obviously strange words come more painlessly to some persons than to others;

STRUCTURAL VISUALIZATION AND LANGUAGE DIFFICULTIES

but as yet the verbal gift eludes laboratory isolation and immediate measurement, only bits of circumstantial evidence occasionally suggesting that lack of the structural aptitude indicates some such inherent endowment. Certainly structural visualization lies idle in language and history courses and when it exceeds other aptitudes may distract a boy from Latin, French, and English.

In a high-school sophomore class, tested through a friend's generosity, Birnie Horgan found individual students ranging

FIGURE 9

BACHELOR OF SCIENCE GRADUATES
AVERAGE HIGH IN STRUCTURAL VISUALIZATION

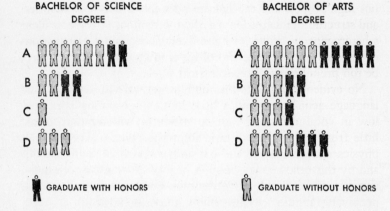

BACHELOR OF SCIENCE DEGREE

BACHELOR OF ARTS DEGREE

GRADUATE WITH HONORS   GRADUATE WITHOUT HONORS

THIS FIGURE SHOWS THE STRUCTURAL-VISUALIZATION GRADES OF 43 MEN WHO GRADUATED IN 1940 FROM A LARGE EASTERN COLLEGE. OF THOSE WITH A BACHELOR OF ARTS DEGREE, 56 PER CENT GRADED A OR B IN STRUCTURAL VISUALIZATION WHEN TESTED BEFORE GRADUATION, IN MANY CASES EVEN BEFORE COLLEGE ENTRANCE, AS COMPARED WITH 50 PER CENT OF AN UNSELECTED MALE POPULATION. OF THOSE WITH A BACHELOR OF SCIENCE DEGREE, 75 PER CENT GRADED A OR B. OF THE LATTER GROUP ALL WHO RECEIVED HONORS GRADED A OR B IN STRUCTURAL VISUALIZATION; WHILE OF THOSE IN ARTS ONE QUARTER GRADED D. SEE FIGURE 16, PAGE 81, FOR THE ACCOUNTING APTITUDE OF THESE SAME STUDENTS.

in age from thirteen to seventeen. The oldest, two years retarded, scored low in both English vocabulary and accounting aptitude but slightly above the average of the class in structural visualization, unmistakably not below. This characteristic, which seems of little classroom help, perhaps a slight hindrance, is too important in twentieth-century adult life to lie idle during the first ten years of formal school.

In a study of college students who graduated in 1940, Julien Weston found those awarded the bachelor-of-science degree averaging higher in structural visualization than those who graduated bachelor of arts, as shown in figure 9. The former may voluntarily elect the sciences; or, an equally plausible explanation, those high in structural visualization may avoid or drop Latin in high school and so of necessity turn away from the bachelor-of-arts degree with its language requirement.

Another conflicting tabulation shows no relation between a student's own estimate of his trouble with Latin and his measured score in structural visualization. This however analyzed a miscellaneous population of two hundred pupils from various high schools and the linkage between language difficulties and structural visualization may be too tenuous to trace in such a heterogeneous group, or more likely an examinee's evaluation of his own performance and of his trouble with a subject may be too prejudiced to have statistical value.

No evidence indicates that high structural visualization aids language acquisition; and a boy, low in accounting aptitude, low in vocabulary, but high in structural visualization, gains little from this engineer's trait before he reaches experimental physics and chemistry, the last year or two of high school; and by this time he may be so disheartened by classroom difficulties that he avoids these exacting courses regarded as oppressively fatiguing by the general school population.

No boy so valuably gifted for the present machine world should reach this stage of discouragement; and yet an incredible number who score high in structural visualization come to the Laboratory with a history of school failure. They tried Latin perhaps freshman year of high school, repeated it once, even twice, and failed; then shifted to French and failed again. To them school work presents an impassable barrier.

22

The full effect on the boy of that normal outlet, a workshop in the basement, to which so many turn, is hard to evaluate. Too much time in this direction may detract from SHOPWORK assigned homework, or a growing love for his shop may foment a distaste for school subjects, or, perhaps the greatest danger of all, unsupervised shopwork in the home may easily instill low standards of accomplishment and contentment with poor quality output.

The Hill School, a private preparatory school for boys, operates a hobby building, the ground floor equipped with excellent machine tools, the second floor for woodworking, the third devoted to art. Here a boy spends whatever free time he wishes under competent workmen, themselves high in structural visualization and accustomed to holding high standards. Dartmouth College recently established a workshop on the same principle. In a large high school a mathematics teacher worked two afternoons a week in the manual-training department on furniture for himself and allowed any boy in the school to work at the same time on his own project providing his standards were high.

Occasionally an independent craftsman runs special classes open to the public, late afternoons and Saturdays, in model-making, bookbinding, photography, or jewelry construction. At one time a professional silversmith hired schoolboys every Saturday afternoon at a nominal rate and insisted on professional standards both because they handled precious metals and because they worked on objects later to be sold. Many an excellent mechanic loves his own trade enough to grasp every chance of handing it on to eager boys.

For the subjective boy, high in finger or tweezer dexterity, directed shopwork gives outlet to structural visualization through the construction of ship models, miniature airplanes, toy railways, and stage sets. But the inclination to illustrate with handwork leads often to a misconception of the characteristic, for one who scores objective in personality does not relish exacting confinement, and turns instead to human problems; while one low in both finger and tweezer dexterity obviously does not enjoy using his hands.

Perhaps one's approach to any problem, one's way of thinking, may be structural. Certainly every boy high in structural visualization should start structural subjects early in school: biology, geology, geometry, solid geometry, and physics. By excelling here he gives the impression of one who should be helped to gain his languages even though difficult of acquisition; for while theoretically a teacher helps every pupil to the utmost, a boy seriously handicapped academically gains a reputation of general incapability. That such a boy scores high in any test seems unbelievable and in consequence a high score in the structural-visualization test is minimized. But one who does well in sciences from the beginning often meets and overcomes the languages with no sense of special inferiority.

III

TECHNICAL VOCABULARIES

Despite incontrovertible reasons for a liberal school background, too many presumably educated persons reach adulthood illiterate in those fields of knowledge for which their aptitudes best equip them. Almost daily a boy, high in structural visualization, proves ignorant of science and destitute of any experience on which to base an intelligent decision.

A college graduate, awarded high academic honors in Greek, tried clerical work in a bank and failed. He next turned to selling for a publishing house and a year and a half later failed again. Tested at this point he scored at the sixtieth percentile in accounting aptitude, high enough to have done his banking job well, and at the sixty-sixth percentile in creative imagination, high enough to have succeeded in selling, except that in addition he scored at the ninety-ninth percentile in structural visualization. Never having taken a single science course, either in high school or college, he had no real shred of evidence on which to base a prejudice that he would not particularly enjoy technical work. Every boy high in structural visualization should get enough technical knowledge to evaluate discerningly the innumerable opportunities open to this type of person.

23

An engineering executive, who asked the Human Engineering Laboratory to test the members of his industrial-research staff,

INDUSTRIAL APPLICATION

found a clearcut pattern of essential aptitudes, together with specific technical knowledge required for survival. He checked these results by having the Laboratory test men he regarded as unsatisfactory; they lacked either the aptitudes or the knowledge of the others. Next he requested the Laboratory to test a number of engineering-school undergraduates from whom he might pick new members for his own organization. Those who showed the correct aptitudes, lacked the technical knowledge he wished; those with adequate knowledge, lacked satisfactory aptitudes.

The ease with which some boys acquire information in any direction misleads them into fields for which they lack the aptitudes. Partly for this reason the Laboratory wishes to test boys first at the age of nine or ten, before they waste too much time acquiring specialized knowledge in a wrong direction; for as the number of industrial organizations which set up their own aptitude patterns gradually increases boys will find it more difficult to obtain work in the field of their acquaintance alone. The Laboratory hopes to guide boys with the aptitudes while they still have sufficient educational time to gain the knowledge they need, for success depends on a rare combination of aptitudes, skill, and knowledge.

24

A thirty-two-page pamphlet by Thomas T. Read, entitled: CAREERS IN THE MINERAL INDUSTRIES, published by the American Institute of Mining and Metallurgical Engineers, 29 West Thirty-ninth Street, New York, gives intelligent insight in this direction. In addition, it lists several pages of books, most of which the high-structural boy should own, and ends with a directory of mineral technological schools, arranged by states, together with the name of the dean, division chairman, or department head, and the special subjects, options, and curricula, offered by each.

MINERAL
INDUSTRIES

25

Aeronautics in general, air conditioning, aircraft, aircraft instruments, airlines operation, airports, alloys, automatic machinery, blast furnaces, boiler design, bookbinding, bulk handling of materials, central-station operation, ceramics, coal, coke ovens, color standardization, conveyors, die casting, diesel engines, elasticity, electric furnaces, electrotyping, elimination of waste, fire prevention, forgings, foundry practice, fuels, gages, gas, gears, heat treatment, hoisting machinery, hydraulic presses, hydraulic turbines, are only a few of several hundred subjects included under mechanical engineering.

DIVISIONS OF
MECHANICAL
ENGINEERING

26

Figure 10 shows at the left the distribution of physics-vocabulary scores for students with one year of high-school physics;
VOCABULARY OF PHYSICS
in the center the distribution for those in their first year of college physics, including a few who have finished one year, and at the right those in their second year of this subject. Ideally every boy high in the aptitude, structural visualization, should work toward scoring equally high in this vocabulary of physics.

Additional knowledge tests, administered by the Laboratory and in which structurally-minded boys should score high, are vocabulary of mathematics, worksample 280, vocabulary of architecture, worksample 250, and vocabulary of medicine, worksample 323.

Most boys high in structural visualization enjoy, even reach eagerly for, the scientific knowledge which underlies these technical vocabularies, often rebelling at the forced acquisition of literature as measured by worksample 293. They should have every opportunity to gain knowledge in the direction which interests them. Knowledge of even so highly specialized a subject as physics seems to carry over and increase general background, enabling one to score higher than otherwise in English vocabulary, for the vocabulary-of-physics test correlates 0.40 with English vocabulary, partly no doubt because we have allowed technical terms to slip into our general tests, but partly also because knowledge of any type seems universally applicable. A boy's every momentary interest should be encouraged and used as incentive to push ahead in that direction with the realization that many such special vocabularies integrate ultimately into a rich unified general background.

Yet despite the importance of knowing one's own field thoroughly, the building of a highly specialized technical knowledge too far above one's general background seems, as judged by statistical findings, wasteful of time and effort, like the piling of blocks, one above another, which must inevitably fall. Rather than push physics, chemistry, engineering, or any isolated subject at the expense of others, a boy can probably more economically raise his general intellectual level.

FIGURE 10

VOCABULARY OF PHYSICS WORKSAMPLE 181 FORM CA

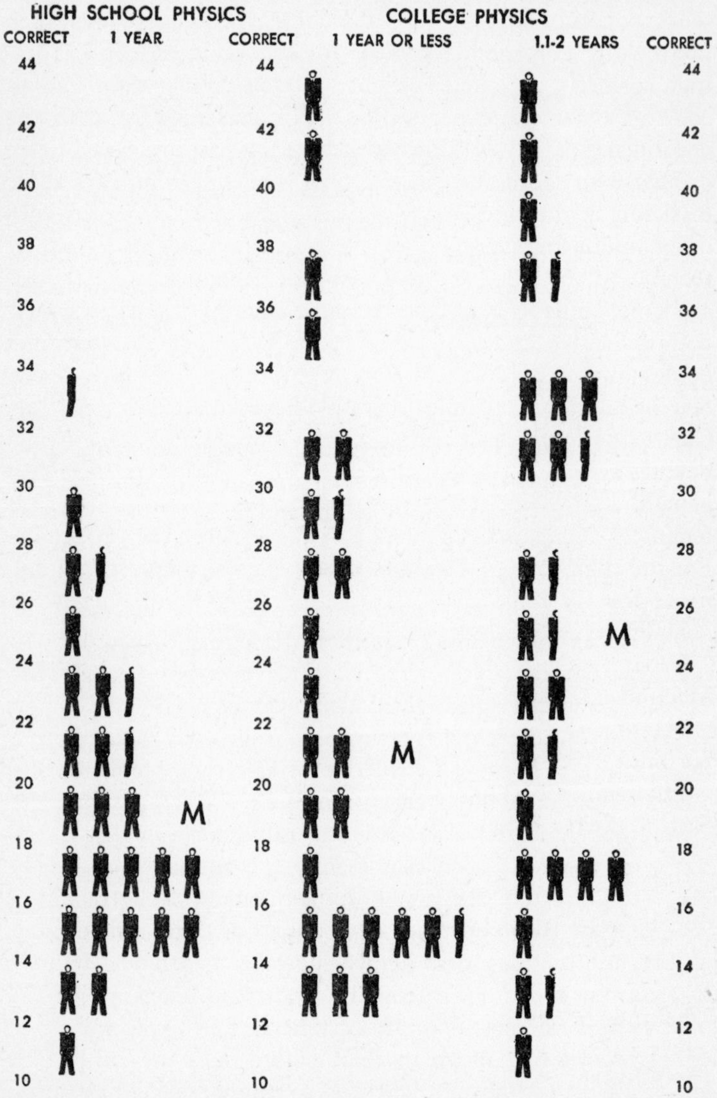

THE GREATEST SINGLE CAUSE OF FAILURE IS LACK OF KNOWLEDGE. FEW PERSONS AP-
PROACH A PERFECT SCORE OF 50 IN THE VOCABULARY-OF-PHYSICS TEST. COLLEGE MEN
AVERAGE HIGHER THAN HIGH-SCHOOL PUPILS BUT NOT SO HIGH AS THEY SHOULD.

No one doubts that engineering-school students work steadily and hard, but careful measurements of results suggest they work less effectively than they might. In explanation of their scoring consistently lower in English-vocabulary tests than presumably comparable students of arts colleges, the Laboratory formerly accepted without question their greater knowledge of technical subjects. Recent experimentation with the vocabulary-of-physics test, worksample 181, shows that of two groups who score alike in this test, academic graduates score markedly higher in general English vocabulary. Coupled with other findings, this implies that engineering students gain their technical knowledge at the expense of other subjects, whereas academic students may gain the same amount as a part of their comprehensive cultural development. With general education comes almost automatically more technical knowledge than one ordinarily realizes. Although technical faculties push so hard as to leave scant time except for details, a student who devotes a specified proportion of his study periods to acquiring general knowledge, bordering on his fields of science, finds technical details coming more easily to justify the procedure. For the engineer and scientist for whom general literature holds no appeal the Laboratory suggests philosophies of science:

DARWINIANA, Thomas H. Huxley; Appleton, 1893.

FROM THE GREEKS TO DARWIN by Henry Fairfield Osborn; Macmillan, 1894; the history of evolution as a scientific concept.

SCIENCE AND THE NEW CIVILIZATION by Robert A. Millikan; Scribner's, 1930.

HISTORY OF SCIENCE AND THE NEW HUMANISM by George Sarton; Henry Holt, 1931; delightful reading.

IV

THE DEXTERITIES

One must be on the alert to distinguish manual dexterity from structural visualization; parents too frequently confuse the two. For the sake of using his hands, a boy may enjoy tinkering with the radio, dismantling an ancient automobile and reassembling it effectively, without belonging in engineering.

27

The reverse happens equally often. A boy low in tweezer dexterity, low in finger dexterity, or in the combination, allows the family clock to stop, the radio to lie idle because of some loose wire, the doorbell to remain useless for want of new batteries, and parents declare him not mechanically inclined, a true assertion in a limited sense of that word; for the mechanic uses his hands and scores high in tweezer dexterity, as does also the draftsman. But the engineer's function is thought; and a boy high in structural visualization, even if low in both tweezer dexterity and finger dexterity, may belong somewhere in the great field called vaguely ENGINEERING, without enjoying manual labor. In large organizations a designing engineer often directs one or more draftsmen who free him entirely from the handling of ruling pens and compasses. He stands at the drawing board for a time each day, watching his ideas materialize on paper, offering suggestions, evading obstacles as they appear, without touching an instrument. As the design approaches completion the engineer may have a mechanic at his disposal, even a small machine shop, to construct his models.

By its own illustrations of ways in which to use structural visualization, the Laboratory adds to the confusion between this trait and manual facility. For to one who scores high in structure it suggests a work bench in the basement, building ship models, bookbinding, sculpture, wood-carving, activities which require hand operations. To the boy who scores high in structural visualization, and who for any reason does not enjoy using his hands, the Laboratory ought to say: think structurally, or some such phrase; structural visualization is a way of thinking, not necessarily of doing. But this is neither vivid nor descriptive. Occasional executives no doubt build their organizations as an architect builds a house; but executives in general score low in structural visualization, not high. The rare salesman may plan his campaigns as an engineer plans a machine; but the group averages clearly low. The man who scores high need not necessarily build with his own hands but should think as do architects, surgeons, and engineers.

FIGURE 11

FINGER DEXTERITY AND THE VIOLIN

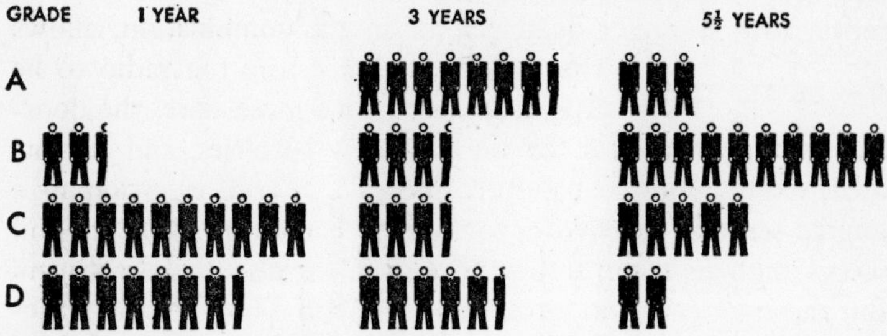

EVERYONE WHO GRADES A IN FINGER DEXTERITY, WHO STUDIES THE VIOLIN, CONTINUES BEYOND THE FIRST YEAR. BOYS AND GIRLS WHO GRADE D SHOULD AVOID THE VIOLIN; FOR COMPARATIVELY FEW OF THIS GROUP WHO START GO ON WITH IT LATER IN LIFE.

A boy low in the dexterities, awkward in handling tools, encounters especial trouble in physics through his clumsiness in manipulating laboratory apparatus. He breaks equipment, ruins the scales, and too easily turns from engineering, without realizing that tweezer dexterity characterizes draftsmen and mechanics, but not necessarily engineers.

28

High finger dexterity, as measured by worksample 16, shows a clear sex difference, occurring more frequently among women than among men; for the comparative distribution between the sexes see THE TOO-MANY-APTITUDE WOMAN, page 48. The gift characterizes meter assemblers, radio assemblers, paper-box makers, and innumerable types of factory operators handling small parts accurately and rapidly. It appears among bank tellers driven at top speed during each noonday rush, but held to exacting precision. It occurs among men and women attracted by photography as a hobby; and to a greater extent among those who continue with the violin beyond the first year.

FINGER DEXTERITY

Figure 11 shows the distribution of finger-dexterity scores among examinees who, at the time of their test, had played the violin for less than a year and, in a majority of instances, stopped,

FIGURE 12

FIELDS SUGGESTED FOR VARIOUS COMBINATIONS OF APTITUDES

				Other Brochures
HIGH CREATIVE IMAGINATION	HIGH STRUCTURAL VISUALIZATION	OBJECTIVE PERSONALITY	OCCUPATIONAL THERAPY, VOCATIONAL TRAINING	TOO-MANY-APTITUDE WOMAN
	HIGH STRUCTURAL VISUALIZATION	EXTREMELY SUBJECTIVE PERSONALITY	ARTS AND CRAFTS, BOOKBINDING, JEWELRY DESIGN, MODEL-THEATER CONSTRUCTION, MUSEUM MOUNTING, SCULPTURE, WOOD-CARVING	TOO-MANY-APTITUDE WOMAN
	AVERAGE OR LOW STRUCTURAL VISUALIZATION	OBJECTIVE PERSONALITY	DEMONSTRATING	TOO-MANY-APTITUDE WOMAN
	AVERAGE OR LOW STRUCTURAL VISUALIZATION	EXTREMELY SUBJECTIVE PERSONALITY	ANATOMY, CHEMICAL ANALYSIS, DENTISTRY, DRAFTING, GLASS BLOWING, MARBLE CUTTING, MECHANICAL CRAFTS, PHYSIOLOGY, SURGERY, WATCH REPAIR	INDIVIDUAL APPROACH TO SCIENTIFIC PROBLEMS
LOW CREATIVE IMAGINATION	HIGH STRUCTURAL VISUALIZATION	HIGH ACCOUNTING APTITUDE	NURSING, NUTRITION (LABORATORY RESEARCH)	UNSOLVED BUSINESS PROBLEMS
	AVERAGE OR LOW STRUCTURAL VISUALIZATION	LOW ACCOUNTING APTITUDE	DENTAL HYGIENE, INSTRUMENT ASSEMBLY, MINIATURE-INSTRUMENT ASSEMBLY, MOUNTING BOTANICAL SLIDES	UNSOLVED BUSINESS PROBLEMS

HIGH TWEEZER DEXTERITY

although some will continue. Note the low finger dexterity of this short-time group, the absence of high scores. The trait alone does not make a violinist; but of those boys and girls sufficiently interested in music to start this instrument only those average or low in finger dexterity became discouraged within the first year. One need but mention singing to show that not all music demands finger dexterity. The natural assumption that boys who continue with the violin acquire finger dexterity is disproved by the distribution of a completely untrained group where exactly the same number grade A and D. Only those who start and stop grade low.

29

Scores in worksample 17, with which the Laboratory formerly measured tweezer dexterity, were independent of finger dexterity, worksample 16. The new tweezer-dex-

TWEEZER
DEXTERITY

terity results, worksample 18, are more reliable than worksample 17, and to this extent an improvement over the earlier test, but correlate (0.36) with finger dexterity, worksample 16. In the course of research, improvement in one direction often does harm in another and is only a step in the long search for perfection.

Fast tweezer-dexterity times, worksample 18, characterize miniature instrument assemblers, surgeons, dentists, watchmakers, glass blowers, and those who handle and set jewels, as suggested in figure 12. Incidentally in these schematic charts the term OBJECTIVE PERSONALITY includes the three divisions of the scale: EXTREMELY OBJECTIVE, OBJECTIVE, and SUBJECTIVE.

30

The tapping test, worksample 221, discussed in UNSOLVED BUSINESS PROBLEMS, shows an exceptionally high reliability (0.95), and requires less than five minutes to administer,

MUSCULAR
SPEED

a rare combination. Solely because the present scoring consumes so much time has the test been removed from the standard battery until some sort of simple machine can be devised for recording and counting the taps.

31

The Laboratory occasionally measures a boy's physical grip, three times with each hand, using a standard dynamometer. The procedure, called worksample 185, shows a satisfactory reliability (0.80) and, except for a correlation of 0.20 with finger dexterity, is distinct from other measures. A score may indicate vaguely a boy's general physical energy, an important element in success; but as yet the staff is no more than collecting data.

GRIP

32

While no precept holds universally true, an objective boy, high in structural visualization, who chances also to score high in either finger dexterity or tweezer dexterity, often attains greater ultimate heights by starting, not in the engineering department, but at a factory assembly job, paid piece-rate. Here he obtains a notion of effective work, of a speed and intensity which schools and colleges rarely convey. In addition he gains first-hand knowledge of factory problems, invaluable later in any engineering position; he becomes acquainted with the working personnel, and often takes an initial step toward a supervisory position. Furthermore every courageous executive faces moments of distressing doubt and insecurity. At such times the man with a tangible trade to which he can return in an emergency, a well-learned skill though never practiced, knows a salutary confidence in himself which comes in no other way. In manufacturing the structurally-minded boy who has operated a lathe with his own hands, assembled instruments, or helped to handle a blast furnace, in printing the boy who has set type or run a press, in the office the boy who has run a business machine, shows an unquestioning confidence in himself, where others fail through worry.

HIGH DEXTERITIES

But no objective boy's full time should go toward these limited skills at the expense of a fuller background essential to executive success. Many mechanically-inclined boys, who advance the idea that by starting as mechanics in modern aviation they will become executives, lack the general knowledge requisite for actual promotion. Objective boys, high in structural visualization, should devote perhaps three quarters of the total year to acquiring formal schooling, needed for executive success, and the remainder to gaining skills. A college student can sometimes get an opportunity to spend a summer in a factory, a foundry, or a machine shop. He can gain a first-hand understanding of airplane mechanics by enrolling for two or three summers in one of the good aviation schools and often finds it a more satisfying vacation than doing nothing. One college graduate, who held a full-time industrial job, arranged with the foreman of the machine shop to run a drill press whenever the department worked overtime. Helped by the older mechanics, who realized his eagerness to learn, he operated every machine in the shop and made lifelong friends among the toolmakers and diemakers of his own organization. He rose rapidly to a major executive position and never directly used his machine-shop knowledge; but its possession gave a confidence which played a substantial part in his success.

v

OBJECTIVE PERSONALITY

Traditional educators classify scientific knowledge as chemical, electrical, mechanical, mining, sanitary, and the like; and technological schools frequently catalogue corresponding engineering departments. Aptitude tests show as yet no clear distinction between these established ramifications, but instead imply a cross classification, for they differentiate the pure scientist, the more practical engineer, the effective manufacturer, and the gregarious salesman, with little regard to the precise product he handles.

The research scientist, happy in his own cloistered workshop, detached from the business world, often scores, in aptitude tests, EXTREMELY SUBJECTIVE. In chemistry he discovered the rare element HELIUM, now of undoubted financial worth but once no more than a laboratory curiosity. In physics he spotted and named Hertzian waves only because they disturbed a sensitive experiment. In aptitudes he tends to score high in structural visualization, often high in inductive reasoning, and subjective or extremely subjective in personality.

The technical engineer, called also the research engineer, grasps the speculative discoveries of the theorist and applies them for the benefit of mankind. His first unwieldy apparatus fills a room, functions only when operated by a corps of assistants, but he demonstrates the utility of the scientist's idea.

TABLE IV

FUNDAMENTAL TRAITS OF TECHNICAL ENGINEERS INCLUDING MECHANICAL AND ELECTRICAL TESTERS AND MAINTENANCE MEN ALSO ENGINEERING SCHOOL STUDENTS

APTITUDE	RATING
STRUCTURAL VISUALIZATION	HIGH
PERSONALITY	SUBJECTIVE OR EXTREMELY SUBJECTIVE

KNOWLEDGE	RATING
VOCABULARY OF PHYSICS	VERY HIGH
VOCABULARY OF MATHEMATICS	VERY HIGH

Next the designing engineer reduces the awkward bulk of this uncertain contraption, simplifying the uncouth snarls in an early radio to the compactness of the modern commercial product. Generally he scores less subjective than the scientist, often near the boundary between the subjective and objective divisions, clearly high in structural visualization, often high in creative imagination, and not necessarily high in inductive reasoning.

The manufacturing executive then produces the engineer's device at a price which the public affords. He scores objective in personality, high in accounting aptitude, often low in both creative imagination and inductive reasoning, and average or above, but not necessarily high, in structural visualization.

The salesman, extremely objective in personality, high in creative imagination, and low in structural visualization, distributes the finished article. Except for a detailed knowledge of his own product the man who sells electrical instruments resembles in aptitudes one who sells chemical and mechanical apparatus, but differs clearly from the pure scientist, at the opposite end of both the personality and structural-visualization scales. Founded on aptitudes alone a boy's decision rests not among the present branches of engineering but first among selling, manufacturing, engineering, and science. If highest in structural visualization and subjective or extremely subjective in personality he should lean toward technical work, if equally high or next highest in inductive reasoning toward pure science, if higher in creative imagination probably toward designing engineering. The objective boy should pick up a general background, not exclusively technical, and aim ultimately toward an executive position in manufacturing.

Regarding the personality scale as continuous from end to end, the scientist, the engineer, the manufacturing executive, and the salesman, correspond crudely to the four artificial divisions: extremely subjective, subjective, objective, and extremely objective. Accepting the bimodality of figure 8, page 40, scientists come from that quarter of the population who score extremely subjective, executives and salesmen from the objective three quarters now called subjective, objective, or extremely objective, while designing engineers come perhaps equally from both. See the schematic chart, figure 13.

33

Selling, advertising, and the influencing of public opinion, which offer opportunities and happiness to extremely objective persons, call specifically for

STRUCTURAL VISUALIZATION AND EXTREME OBJECTIVITY

low scores in the structural-visualization tests; and accordingly an extremely objective examinee who scores no more than average in this last trait succeeds probably more often than one who scores high, despite everyone's desire to rank at the top in every test. Designing engineering, scientific research, and surgery, demand high structural visualization but are most congenial to those subjective or extremely subjective in per-

FIGURE 13

Suggestions for Various Combinations of Aptitudes

EXTREMELY OBJECTIVE, OBJECTIVE, AND PERHAPS SUBJECTIVE PERSONALITY

Inductive Reasoning	Structural Visualization	Creative Imagination / Accounting Aptitude	Suggestions	Other Brochures
HIGH INDUCTIVE REASONING	HIGH STRUCTURAL VISUALIZATION	HIGH CREATIVE IMAGINATION	CITY PLANNING, SLUM CLEARANCE	TOO-MANY-APTITUDE WOMAN
		LOW CREATIVE IMAGINATION	DIRECTING ARCHAEOLOGICAL EXPEDITIONS	
	LOW STRUCTURAL VISUALIZATION	HIGH CREATIVE IMAGINATION	ADULT EDUCATION SUPERVISION, ADVERTISING, EDITORIAL WORK, PUBLISHING, PUBLIC HEALTH	OBJECTIVE APPROACH TO GROUP-INFLUENCING FIELDS
		LOW CREATIVE IMAGINATION	DEPARTMENT-STORE COMPLAINT WORK, DIPLOMACY, POLITICS	UNSOLVED BUSINESS PROBLEMS
LOW INDUCTIVE REASONING	AVERAGE STRUCTURAL VISUALIZATION	HIGH ACCOUNTING APTITUDE	MANUFACTURING EXECUTIVE WORK, ENGINEERING EXECUTIVE WORK, FACTORY MANAGEMENT	
		HIGH CREATIVE IMAGINATION	SALES ENGINEERING, SELLING HEAVY GOODS	
	LOW STRUCTURAL VISUALIZATION	HIGH ACCOUNTING APTITUDE	BUILDING MANAGEMENT, BUSINESS MANAGEMENT, CITY MANAGEMENT, DINING HALL SUPERVISION, EXECUTIVE WORK, HOSPITAL MANAGEMENT, HOUSING MANAGEMENT, MUSEUM MANAGEMENT, STORE MANAGEMENT	UNSOLVED BUSINESS PROBLEMS
		HIGH CREATIVE IMAGINATION	MERCHANDIZING, BOND SELLING, SALES PROMOTION, STORE SELLING	OBJECTIVE APPROACH TO GROUP-INFLUENCING FIELDS

FIGURE 13 (CONTINUED)

SUGGESTIONS FOR VARIOUS COMBINATIONS OF APTITUDES

					Other Brochures
EXTREMELY SUBJECTIVE PERSONALITY PERHAPS SUBJECTIVE PERSONALITY	HIGH INDUCTIVE REASONING	HIGH STRUCTURAL VISUALIZATION	HIGH CREATIVE IMAGINATION	MEDICAL RESEARCH SCIENTIFIC RESEARCH	INDIVIDUAL APPROACH TO SCIENTIFIC PROBLEMS
EXTREMELY SUBJECTIVE PERSONALITY PERHAPS SUBJECTIVE PERSONALITY	HIGH INDUCTIVE REASONING	HIGH STRUCTURAL VISUALIZATION	LOW CREATIVE IMAGINATION	DIAGNOSTIC MEDICINE PATENT LAW PHYSIOLOGICAL CHEMISTRY PALEOBOTANY	INDIVIDUAL APPROACH TO SCIENTIFIC PROBLEMS
EXTREMELY SUBJECTIVE PERSONALITY PERHAPS SUBJECTIVE PERSONALITY	HIGH INDUCTIVE REASONING	LOW STRUCTURAL VISUALIZATION	LOW CREATIVE IMAGINATION	BOOK REVIEWING CRIMINAL LAW HISTORICAL WRITING REPORT WRITING REWRITE WORK	CHARACTERISTICS COMMON TO PROFESSIONAL MEN IN NON-STRUCTURAL FIELDS
EXTREMELY SUBJECTIVE PERSONALITY PERHAPS SUBJECTIVE PERSONALITY	LOW INDUCTIVE REASONING	HIGH STRUCTURAL VISUALIZATION	HIGH FINGER DEXTERITY	HOSPITAL LABORATORY WORK	TOO-MANY-APTITUDE WOMAN
EXTREMELY SUBJECTIVE PERSONALITY PERHAPS SUBJECTIVE PERSONALITY	LOW INDUCTIVE REASONING	HIGH STRUCTURAL VISUALIZATION	HIGH CREATIVE IMAGINATION	TECHNICAL ENGINEERING AMPLIFIER DESIGN BROADCASTING APPARATUS DESIGN	CHARACTERISTICS COMMON TO TECHNICAL ENGINEERS
EXTREMELY SUBJECTIVE PERSONALITY PERHAPS SUBJECTIVE PERSONALITY	LOW INDUCTIVE REASONING	LOW STRUCTURAL VISUALIZATION	HIGH CREATIVE IMAGINATION	ACTING IMAGINATIVE WRITING	UNSOLVED BUSINESS PROBLEMS

sonality. Toolmakers, diemakers, machine-setup men, and skilled mechanics, who continue their trade happily through life, score most frequently extremely subjective.

34

One exception, architecture, seems to involve both design and supervision. For the former the architect needs structural visualization, while to handle plumbers, painters, carpenters, and contractors, he needs the characteristics of the executive. But the architect in addition scores high in creative imagination and the boy without this trait should probably avoid the field. See THE TOO-MANY-APTITUDE WOMAN which discusses architecture at too great length to repeat here and which also gives distribution curves for three forms of the vocabulary-of-architecture test, worksample 250.

ARCHITECTURE

35

Ordained medicine gives no natural outlet for extreme objectivity coupled with high structural visualization, for the doctor's human contacts are both personal and professional and more satisfying to the subjective than to the objective person. If medicine abandons its individual approach and turns to public health more than today, or in some extreme eventuality becomes a government-controlled enterprise, a new combination of characteristics will no doubt enter. But at present a boy who scores extremely objective in personality and high in structural visualization should view skeptically any suggestion that he enter medicine. Men who, each year as they grow older, make sounder places for themselves in surgery tend to score extremely subjective; for objectivity demands more social contacts than the operating room allows, more even than seem to enter private practice.

MEDICINE AND OBJECTIVITY

In the normal course of appointments four surgeons, high in structural visualization and extremely objective in personality, came to the Laboratory with virtually the same complaint; they held established places in surgery or private medicine but felt restless and dissatisfied with their own lives. To use his objectivity one of the four accepted the executive management of a New York hospital but now misses the challenge of structural problems and does not recommend the decision as ideal. Another became dean of a medical school and now feels equally impatient to use his structural visualization. A third has found what seems a happier outcome by continuing surgery and in addition teaching part-time in medical school. Perhaps the most satisfying solution is that of the fourth man who continues his surgical practice and handles in addition a public evening clinic which he organized as an outlet for his objectivity.

36

A host of current jobs call for irrational aptitude patterns. The self-contradictory name SALES ENGINEERING dooms to failure

SALES ENGINEERING
one who accepts the title as a goal, for engineering demands high structural visualization, successful selling a low score in the same trait; and no one ranks simultaneously at opposite ends of any scale. Nor does an average grade between the extremes settle the dilemma, for gradually accumulating evidence suggests that each person will prove ultimately of either one type or the other, either high in structural visualization or low, and never between.

The effective sales engineer ignores the term and develops his own approach. If high in structural visualization he collects customers who turn to him for technical advice, acts primarily as a consulting engineer and although often responsible for as many actual sales as any salesman he develops a technique for appearing to accept only orders thrust upon him; when the time comes for the binding signature he turns the transaction over to some clerk in his own sales department.

Another so-called sales engineer, low in structural visualization but objective or extremely objective in personality, attacks his job as a salesman, makes the first approach to the prospective customer and finally watches the contract signed, counting on the engineering department of his organization to settle technical questions. These diverse individuals, the high-structural, perhaps subjective engineer and the objective, low-structural salesman, may sell annually the same volume, but each, thinking in terms of ultimate accomplishment, refashions his task, consciously or unconsciously, to suit his aptitudes. Either man forced by circumstances in any direction, toward law, science, or the fine arts, would probably have applied his native aptitudes in some similar fashion and succeeded as well.

37

A manufacturer and distributor of farm implements divides the problem of rural merchandizing into selling, mechanical servicing, and the administration of sales agencies including their financing, and declares that the same person rarely both sells and services well, a conclusion readily explicable on the basis of test results, for selling demands an objective personality coupled with low structural visualization, while effective mechanical servicing and the upkeep of farm tools demand a high score in the last together with subjectivity.

SELLING AND SERVICING
AGRICULTURAL IMPLEMENTS

An objective or extremely objective boy, high in the structural aptitudes and attracted by selling, should operate his own sales agency, directing personally the mechanical servicing of his product, vital to continued success in any rural community. He should give individual farmers his best technical and professional advice, act as an affable, unpaid farm consultant, and hire salesmen to take his orders, for a man high in structural visualization rarely gets, as salesmen say, the name on the dotted line. One such man scrupulously avoids even accepting orders, invariably replying that he will send a salesman around.

38

A trained farm advisor serves his clients much as any private engineering consultant, charging a professional fee for his counsel. He knows soil chemistry and the effect of various fertilizers, follows the market and suggests profitable ventures, understands the rotation of crops, spraying, and the care of fruit trees, animal hus-

FARM ADVISOR

bandry, and breeding. A counselor in the middle west receives an annual retaining fee from a number of neighboring farms, each more successful because of his help, but no one of which could afford a full-time scientist.

This seems an ideal opportunity for an objective boy, high in structural visualization, who enjoys animals and the out-of-doors. But the work requires limitless knowledge of plants, insects, and the weather. Too often a boy owns a dog, rabbits, guinea pigs, or white mice, with no real knowledge of their care. At the age of nine he should start a library with a book on each of the following subjects: ants, bees, birds, breeding, cows, farms, grains, heredity, horses, insects, poultry, pumps, pruning, roads, and wells. To own a thousand volumes by the time a boy graduates from college, not too large a library for the modern farm consultant, means beginning at the age of nine or ten and collecting two books a week for ten years.

39

The ultimate aim of the state employee doing farm extension work parallels exactly that of the professional farm advisor but his aptitudes probably differ. The private FARM EXTENSION consultant focuses his attention exclusively on the problem at hand for he serves a client who pays for his help and recognizes the value of his services. The state-extension worker may encounter any problem in the course of his rounds but his primary responsibility is teaching the application of recognized processes or the use of labor-saving tools already proved of value in more progressive communities, for his aim is to help backward farms, which do not realize their own need for assistance. The farm-extension worker scores therefore more like the teacher and less like the scientist, highest in creative imagination, next highest in inductive reasoning, and perhaps third highest in structural visualization.

A single comprehensive volume, too difficult for a boy to read uninterruptedly but which should betimes hold a prominent place on his shelves for handy reference, is:

THE SCIENCE OF LIFE, in two volumes, by H. G. Wells, Julian S. Huxley, and G. P. Wells; Doubleday, Doran, 1931.

40

Scientific forestry no doubt demands structural visualization, and for a time the boy who scores high is happy in this direction. But advancement too often sweeps him to an office-supervisory position, which gives the structural aptitude little opportunity. As in surgery an extremely subjective person enjoys forestry research and achieves a place in the scientific aspects of the work; but an objective boy, almost despite himself, ends at a government desk.

FORESTRY

41

As engineers score more frequently high than low in structural visualization, and managers, superintendents, and foremen, average objective, executives in the broad field covered by the ambiguous term ENGINEERING presumably unite the two mathematically independent traits. The so-called consulting engineer employs structural visualization in solving the same constructural problems as the technical or designing engineer; in addition he uses an objective personality in renting his own office, handling his own accounts, selling his services, and ultimately in managing a staff consisting first of a secretary and finally of draftsmen, clerks, junior engineers, and perhaps associates, differing thus from the man who works under explicit instructions for an assured salary. The consulting chemist faces a parallel problem, as may also the executive director of a research laboratory.

CONSULTING ENGINEERS

To gain so notable a position the ambitious boy who scores simultaneously high in structural visualization and objective in personality should prepare thoroughly for two often mutually exclusive approaches. He needs, first, sound technical or engineering knowledge and, second, an equally sound executive background.

Edmund V. Cowdry, in his provocative preface to HUMAN BIOLOGY AND RACIAL WELFARE, describes the perpetual conflict between epical scientific discoveries, the outcome frequently of extreme specialization, and the integration of cumulative knowledge, the intelligent building of a unified structure, demanding breadth of cultural background. A similar clash appears in the Laboratory's counsel; with the structurally-minded boy it recommends laboratory courses in the exact sciences, while with one who scores objective or extremely objective it advises against specialization and urges a full, rich education. Ideally, the boy with whom these traits combine needs both types of training, and to approach so utopian a goal must begin early in life.

Even before such a boy reads with ease, certainly before he grasps every concept of the printed page, parents should surround him with a scientific reference library, at hand whenever the mood impels, extensive enough to answer each momentary query. Frequently a father objects: ' But you have not read the book I gave you last! ', implicitly suggesting specialization, implying that a boy digest one volume, learn an isolated subject as presented by an individual author, before starting on another. A child assimilates aspects of a book, perhaps at first the pictures, possibly the diagrams, sometimes the first few prefatory chapters, before he understands the entire text; for material of widely varying intellectual levels, concepts familiar to every enlightened adult, followed by abstruse philosophies, appear in many volumes. If objective, the developing boy should absorb essential bits from each of several books before he reads one to the end; he should integrate knowledge, add as he feels inspired, gather simultaneously from multifarious books, not be forced to acquire information in its present-day often artificial compartments.

Texts admittedly beyond the primary student should line his own shelves rather than be absent when a question occurs, blocking him from the fact he wants with the recurrent danger that the opportune moment passes unsatisfied. Parents and teachers continually underestimate the child's capacity, his intellectual curiosity and breadth of interest, persistently retarding him, for when they finally sense his needs he has already grown beyond. Even colleges limit the library a boy can own by insisting that he empty his room each spring so that a summer-school student can move in. One who plans on consulting, which demands encyclopedic knowledge, should inquire in advance and avoid institutions with this regulation.

The structurally-minded boy should grow again with each science. He thinks as did those who made the original advances, rarely as current historians describing the past. For him source material, not at first of remote antiquity, presents the discoveries of three or four decades or half a century past with an alive interest; while expensive modern texts, even when written by scientists, expatiate on recent trends, reviewing the past superficially, merely for the sake of completeness.

Viewed from another angle, a child's first genuine interest in a book as a personal possession may come through finding on the fly-leaf the autograph of some distinguished prior owner; and as the wealthier schools and colleges keep their own libraries up-to-date, selling a book only a few years old to buy a new edition, textbooks of the past are often much less expensive than modern editions.

Both high-school and college teachers overlook the benefits of old editions, and require the purchase of recent texts, out of date again before the boy graduates, often not so lasting as earlier ones, and bought at a price which precludes other books; the accumulation of a comprehensive library requires not only years of intelligent selection but money. Perhaps too few teachers realize the practicability of buying a sufficient quantity of both new and used copies of many old editions for every member of a class to own the same printing, with identical page references, and at so low a price that a teacher may require parallel texts by other authorities. The present writer has known a boy to fail a school subject with one text which became perfectly clear with another; for every author possesses a combination of aptitudes peculiar to himself and may as a result be immediately intelligible to boys who resemble him and unintelligible to those who differ.

Each boy must set his own goal of accomplishment, for no one can define SUCCESS or HAPPINESS for another. Galton picks one man in every 4,000 as eminent, and the boy who aspires to this level should score above 4,000 others in a knowledge of his field. For convenience in placing him in comparison with others the Laboratory administers several technical vocabulary tests, mathematics, physics, and medicine, subjects which should be familiar to the structurally-minded person.

42

The objective youth, high in structural visualization, has before him at least three college options. In pursuance of
FURTHER
EDUCATION
further education he may select a business administration course in an engineering or technical school and so obtain both his executive and engineering training in four undergraduate years. For entrance he needs trigonometry and solid geometry, as well as high-school physics and chemistry. During his first college year he takes the same courses as his technical classmates, but either at the beginning or in the middle of sophomore year turns gradually toward business subjects. The boy who seems most successful from this point on grades B in structural visualization and average or above in accounting aptitude. Such a boy often encounters trouble in freshman year with the technical subjects required but if willing to work finds his objective personality and accounting aptitude more important thereafter than his lower structural visualization. See table VIII for a list of engineering schools many of which offer such business-training courses.

Another boy higher in structural visualization, grade A or B+ men's norms, may elect a four-year engineering course in such a technical school as those listed in table VIII, obtaining a thorough technical training as an undergraduate, and capping this with one or two years of business administration in a graduate school, his undergraduate work fitting him for engineering, his graduate course for an executive position.

Still another who, despite high structural visualization, finds scholarship not too laborious may start with a four-year academic college course, thus gaining the general background needed for executive success, and follow with graduate work in engineering. In a few arts colleges he may leave at the end of his third year to commence his engineering course and if successful return to graduate with his academic classmates.

Each of these proposals has its merits. The last two, six or seven years of education, give of necessity more vocabulary than the four years of the first. The last choice begins with a general background which contributes to the ease and efficiency of acquiring technical knowledge thereafter; but four years of purely academic work are often extremely discouraging for the boy high in structural visualization.

As compared with boys' liberal arts colleges, practically all engineering schools are recently founded. Of the former the oldest third date from Harvard University founded in 1636 to Bowdoin College in Brunswick, Maine, founded in 1794; the newest third date from Emory University in Atlanta, 1836, to Northeastern University in Boston, 1898. Of the engineering schools, only one of those listed is older than the newest third of men's colleges, the oldest third ranging from 1824 to 1879. As discussed later under AGE OF COLLEGE, page 136, the newness of the engineering schools may contribute to their low vocabularies. There seems at least some statistical suggestion that boys high in vocabulary tend to drop out of engineering schools for what are termed personal reasons, perhaps because they are not fully challenged.

In brief, the first of these three programs, a business administration course in an engineering school, gives the objective boy, who scores average or high in structural visualization, an opportunity to obtain both engineering and executive training as an undergraduate in a period of four years, and after freshman year to use simultaneously his structural visualization and objective personality. Four years of engineering followed by graduate work in business school challenges high structural visualization probably more than the other programs. The third, three or four years of academic work, followed by graduate work in engineering, challenges most fully the high vocabulary student.

43

Restless high-school seniors and conscientious parents daily ask members of the Laboratory staff the advisability of a boy's going to work instead of to college. While a youthful, energetic boy, releasing his pent-up structural visualization, forges rapidly ahead in industry, he soon reaches a plateau limited by his vocabulary. Recently, a large business organization listed with great care the names of

WORK OR COLLEGE

present employees who for some reason have never fulfilled the promise with which they started and who are now carried on the company's payroll only because of their years of service. When tested, the men on this list scored high in aptitudes but low in vocabulary, for ultimate executive success, toward which the objective boy strives, correlates more closely with English vocabulary than with any other single measurable trait. By the time a boy senses his need he feels too old to return to college and continue vocabulary building, or has responsibilities which hold him to his job. While one can without doubt add vocabulary at any time of life, few do it. Most need the drive of formal schooling.

VI

BEHAVIOR

Now and then an objective or even extremely objective boy, as judged by the word-association test, avoids social functions, enjoys working alone, looks forward to research, and cannot picture himself as an executive gaining the cooperation of classmates, dealing satisfactorily with people. He believes himself extremely subjective despite the test score and in the opinion of both parents and teachers behaves subjectively.

PERSONALITY, in the Laboratory's terminology, designates specifically the trait measured by the word-association test scored on statistically significant responses, a minute fraction of what is ordinarily regarded as personality in the more general sense. After 14, the trait shows no change with age or experience and little change before that point. There exists however another side of the total personality, which clearly changes with experience, and which the Laboratory terms BEHAVIOR. Because one sees this aspect, one comes almost inevitably to judge inherent PERSONALITY by apparent BEHAVIOR.

With the boy who thinks himself extremely subjective and whose parents confirm this viewpoint the word-association score may always be in error. But in the minds of most members of the Laboratory staff, especially those familiar with the results of this test over a period of years, its inaccuracy is the least likely alternative. As a boy high in structural visualization may know nothing of either science or engineering, so one who scores objective in personality may have little experience in handling and directing others or in meeting strangers, not enough to feel at ease or to know with any certainty the chances of ultimate enjoyment.

While no one should precipitously elect high-pressure selling as a life's work against his own best judgment, just because he scores objective in personality, he should nevertheless use this score as an indication that he may find more pleasure in social contacts than he expects, and should seek some degree of social experience. If he can afford the dues he should join a school, college, or university club. He should investigate the social groups open to both men and women and listed in the Laboratory's brochure: THE TOO-MANY-APTITUDE WOMAN. If high in structural visualization he should join a science or engineering society.

For boys and girls ages 12 to 18:

American Institute of the City of New York, 60 East Forty-second Street, New York City. Write this organization for its booklet: HOW TO ORGANIZE A SCIENCE CLUB, price 25 cents. It includes an excellent list of two hundred books for a boy's science library. Because to collect these, even as rapidly as one a week, requires four years, the Laboratory urges an objective boy, high in structural visualization, who should own personally for ready reference most of these books, to begin early building his own library. The American Institute Science and Engineering Clubs, in cooperation with the American Museum of Natural History, holds an annual Science and Engineering Fair. Junior exhibitors are from 12 to 14 years of age, senior exhibitors from 15 to 18. The Institute classifies exhibits as:

1. Biological Sciences

Plants and Animals—their relation to their environment; structure and function.

Medicine and Bio-Chemistry—the human body in sickness and health and the relation of chemistry to biology.

Heredity and Evolution—the betterment of the race through the study of genetics.

II. Physical Sciences

Our place in the Universe—geology, physical geography, meteorology, and astronomy—a search into the physical manifestations around us.

Physics—the applications of physical laws.

Chemistry—modern techniques and their contributions.

III. Engineering

Transportation and Distribution—principles involved in the making of airplanes, automobiles, ships, warehouses.

Communication—speech, radio, television, movies, print, teletype, and telephone.

Production—raw materials and the help of science in using them for manufacture and agriculture.

Public Welfare—conservation, housing, city planning, and public health as affected by scientific discoveries.

IV. Research

A portrayal of a systematic investigation of some phenomenon by the experimental method to discover facts or to coordinate them as laws.

For boys and girls ages 11 to 18:

The American Institute Science and Engineering Clubs hold also an annual Scholastic Salon of Photography; junior entries open to ages 11 to 14, senior entries 15 to 18.

For college students:

American Institute of Chemical Engineers, Chemists Building, New York City, had in June, 1934, thirty-seven student chapters with a total membership of 1,897 college students.

American Institute of Electrical Engineers, headquarters: 33 West Thirty-ninth Street, New York City, a national organization, founded in 1884, to advance the theory and practice of electrical engineering. Membership, October 1, 1940, 17,890. Its seventeen technical committees include: air transportation, automatic stations, basic sciences, communication, domestic and commercial applications, education, electric welding, electrical machinery, electrochemistry, and electrometallurgy, industrial power applications, instruments and measurements, land transportation, production and application of light, marine transportation, power generation, power transmission and distribution, and protective devices.

American Institute of Mining and Metallurgical Engineers, Engineering Societies Building, 29 West Thirty-ninth Street, New York City. An undergraduate or graduate college student may be a student associate. This society publishes: CAREERS IN THE MINERAL INDUSTRIES by Thomas T. Read, discussed on page 48.

American Society of Mechanical Engineers, Engineering Societies Building, 20 West Thirty-ninth Street, New York City; also mid-west office: Engineering Building, 205 West Wacker Drive, Chicago. Student members, now 7,000 in number, must be enrolled in an engineering course in one of the 117 schools which has a student branch of the society. Student annual dues, $3.00. Junior members must have graduated in engineering. Junior initiation fee $10.00; junior annual dues, $10.00.

With social experience comes almost invariably a type of behavior which the world regards as belonging to one who scores objective in personality, greater confidence, more self-assurance in social situations, without however a change in the word-association score or in the inherent personality which that test betrays. One who originally scores objective often develops an unexpected enjoyment of society and sometimes what seems a more satisfactory adjustment to life.

VII

ACCOUNTING APTITUDE

Twenty-two college graduates who, after careful consideration, applied to a small city bank for permanent employment scattered widely in accounting aptitude, from low *D's* to high *A's*. Of the entire group, seventeen, if hired, must leave within five years to render the remaining five as carefully selected as are the present employees of the same bank of whom ninety per cent grade high. Even college men, with presumably every opportunity to consider their own vocational futures over a period of years, seek work so ill-advisedly that in this instance 17 out of 22 would hold the jobs they take less than five years. In fact, 8 of the 22 applicants were hired and not one lasted two years. Their elders like to think of those who apply for a

FIGURE 14

GROWTH OF ACCOUNTING APTITUDE (WORKSAMPLE 1)
COMPARISON OF MEN AND WOMEN

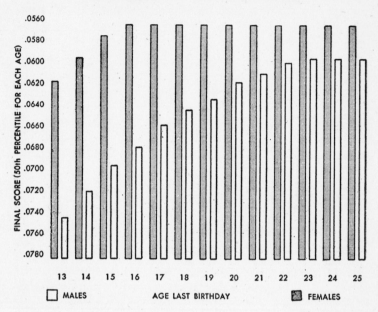

THROUGH THE HIGH-SCHOOL YEARS BOYS WORK AT A DISADVANTAGE IN ALL STUDIES WHICH REQUIRE ACCOUNTING APTITUDE, FOR THEY START LOW AND GROW SLOWLY FROM AGE 13 TO 23. GIRLS AT THE AGE OF 13 SCORE COLLECTIVELY HIGHER THAN BOYS AND MATURE AT 16.

life's occupation as doing so intelligently, after facing their own future aspirations. Instead many men, both youths and adults, enter fields where from the beginning they are doomed to ultimate failure.

Sanguine parents assume that low-accounting-aptitude boys acquire the trait with daily experience in banking; but the youngest of these applicants exceeded twenty-two and a minute study of accounting aptitude extending over twenty years and based upon the measurements of thirty thousand persons shows no measurable change after twenty-three.

The constancy of number-checking scores from this age to thirty-five leads the Laboratory to believe that accounting aptitude, as measured by worksamples 1 and 268, is largely unaffected by education. On the assumption that performance depends upon training one would expect scores to improve, for much professional training in accountancy comes after twenty-three. The actual curves for men and women, figure 14, seem more consistent with an accounting aptitude which grows with age rather than with education and experience.

44

A recent word-checking test, worksample 267 with which an appointment often starts, proves an excellent introduction, helping to explain subsequent and somewhat ACCOUNTING- similar tasks in the battery and going rapidly APTITUDE TESTS enough to set a fast pace, important at the outset because scores so consistently depend upon speed. But the results correlate too closely with English vocabulary (0.39, STATISTICAL BULLETIN 475) to indicate inherent aptitude free from acquired knowledge.

Another recent accounting-aptitude test, worksample 268, presents two columns of numbers in place of words. Identical in format with worksample 267, it contains a vertical space in the center headed SAME where the examinee checks when the components of the item agree. Form A, the first of six, contains three-digit numbers; form B, four digits; form C, five; to form F with eight-digit numbers. To save testing time, annually more at a premium as the known aptitudes increase, the last forms, E and F, may be omitted.

At the time of writing, the number-checking test, worksample 268, gives the most accurate evaluation of accounting aptitude as distinct from other traits (reliability=0.93, STATISTICAL BULLETIN 658). Occasionally administrators still give worksample 1, with a reliability of only 0.80 (STATISTICAL BULLETIN 53), largely because most of the studies reported in this brochure are based on that primitive number-checking test.

An early consonant-checking test, worksample 187, proved in one study to contain fewer factors than worksample 1 which it paralleled. Following this, worksample 269, which contains consonants only and for which test administrators are now collecting data, may finally surpass the new number checking.

45

For those interested in the details of the Laboratory's research, table v shows the freedom of accounting aptitude as measured by worksample 268 from other traits. A cor-

INDEPENDENCE
OF TRAITS

relation of zero (0.00), almost never found, represents complete independence, one of 0.10 or less is satisfactorily low. For years the staff has tried unsuccessfully to reduce the correlation of 0.24, the highest of the list, between accounting aptitude and inductive reasoning.

TABLE V

Correlation of Accounting Aptitude, Worksample 268 with:

Personality, Worksample 35	0.02
Structural Visualization, Worksample 4	0.02
Pitch Discrimination, Worksample 76	0.06
Structural Visualization, Worksample 5	0.09
Structural Visualization, Worksample 204 A	0.10
Observation, Worksample 206 CA	0.10
Analytical Reasoning, Worksample 244 CA	0.14
Tweezer Dexterity, Worksample 18	0.14
Creative Imagination, Worksample 161 (group)	0.14
Finger Dexterity, Worksample 16	0.19
Creative Imagination, Worksample 161 (individual)	0.24
Inductive Reasoning, Worksample 164 FA	0.24

46

A boy higher in accounting aptitude than in any other trait who uses the gift as an essential part of his work gains greater success than one who ignores it. He should ac-

USE OF
ACCOUNTING
APTITUDE

quire a grasp of statistics as a tool for approaching the study of population problems and of heredity, as discussed in the Laboratory's bro-

chure: THE TOO-MANY-APTITUDE WOMAN, presented there because women as a group average above men in accounting aptitude and more often face the necessity of using the

FIGURE 15

A CHANCE GROUP OF PUBLIC HIGH SCHOOL STUDENTS

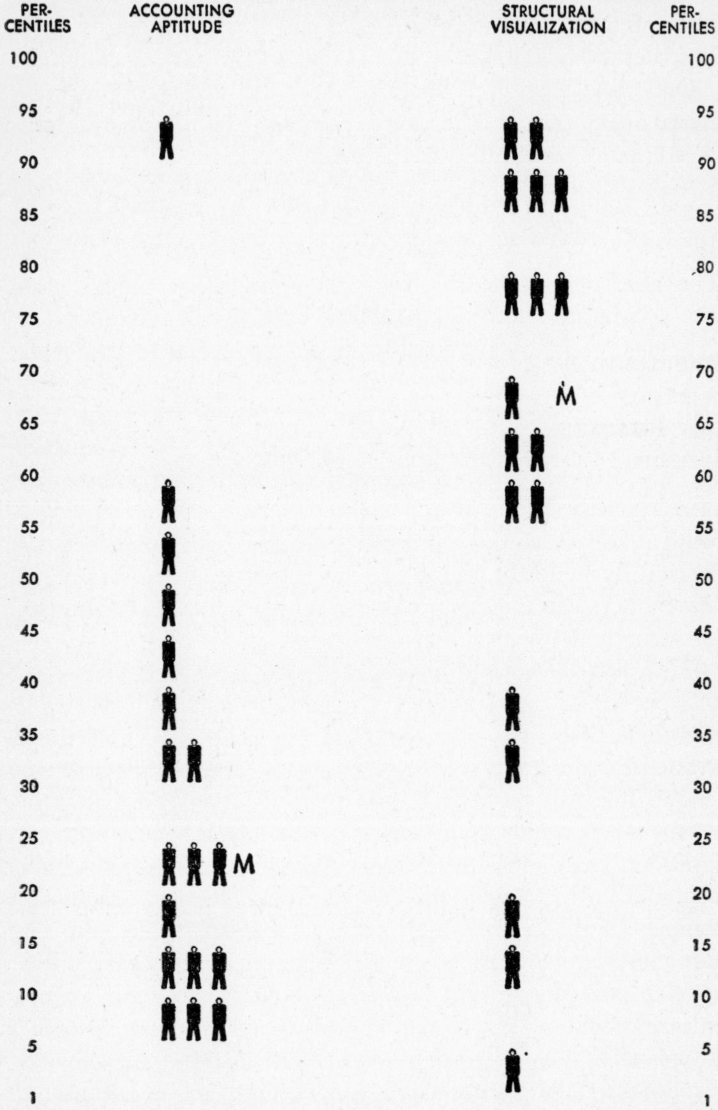

THIS GROUP HAPPENS TO SCORE LOW IN ACCOUNTING APTITUDE AND HIGH IN STRUCTURAL VISUALIZATION. MOST OF THESE STUDENTS SHOULD TAKE GEOMETRY BEFORE ALGEBRA.

trait consciously. He should study accounting as mentioned in UNSOLVED BUSINESS PROBLEMS, written for the objective adult high in accounting aptitude, and if simultaneously high in structural visualization should investigate cost accounting.

Only one low in accounting aptitude becomes painfully aware of the trait as a necessity and of the hardships which its lack imposes, especially in classroom work.

47

The academic obstacles structural visualization joined with low accounting aptitude, divert the scientifically minded boy

STRUCTURAL VISU-
ALIZATION AND
LOW ACCOUNTING
APTITUDE

by cumulative degrees from his legitimate environment. In the early grades he meets arithmetic and fails through slowness with figures, or succeeds only by austerities which inculcate an enduring distaste for all mathematics. In high school he begins algebra, further dependent on accounting aptitude, and again fails or detests the subject. By junior or senior year his acquired aversion to numbers induces the avoidance of all exact sciences, normal outlets for structural visualization.

For a fifteen-year-old boy who graded A, at the ninety-second percentile, in structural visualization and D, below the twentieth percentile, in accounting aptitude the Laboratory stressed the desirability of both geometry and physics in high school. But an experienced principal, accurate and fast with his own paper-and-pencil activities and low in the structural aptitude, regarded the sciences as the stiffest doses of the curriculum. To the boy's father he explained the avowed shortcomings of the Human-Engineering-Laboratory tests and felt that a boy so obviously below par in mathematics could hardly hope to pass physics and certainly would fail to make an engineering school. He recommended typing and stenography as less scholastic and finally, with the best intentions, allowed the boy to take chemistry, a science least apt as ordinarily taught in its elementary stages to use structural visualization. The boy graduated without the minimum requirements for engineering, unable to enter an academic school where he might take science courses, and at the time of writing these pages has just been asked, at the end of five months, to leave the business school where he enrolled.

The Human Engineering Laboratory knows mathematically the inaccuracies of its measurements. The chances that letter grade A in the wiggly block is grossly in error are about 2 in 100, as shown by the correlation with other structural work-samples. (See TECHNICAL REPORTS 13, 14, and 18.) The chances of its being correct or a close approximation to the truth are probably better than 80 in 100; and by the administration of several structural tests the Laboratory betters this accuracy. But every teacher and school principal should stress known errors so that no boy banks too heavily on aptitude results. On the other hand, granting possible error, the boy in question, now 19, passed chemistry with ease but has never tried geometry, physics, or any highly structural science, and even a general education should include one of these subjects.

This detailed case history typifies the experiences of many students high in structural visualization and low in accounting aptitude. They labor through arithmetic, repeat algebra demanded by a majority of high schools as preparation for geometry, and so never try the latter subject, a lack which bars them from experimental physics.

Statistically one boy in sixteen grades A in structural visualization and D in accounting aptitude, a sufficient percentage of extreme cases to justify every large school in offering, as do a few now, a specially planned course presenting geometry before algebra in such a way as not to demand the latter subject. Though a boy low in accounting aptitude encounters some trouble with both, he finds geometry the easier, and if he does well starts algebra with more confidence, not beaten at the outset by his low accounting aptitude. He also approaches algebra with an additional year of mathematical experience behind him, and with an accounting aptitude, still growing at this age, a year more mature. The structurally-minded boy, not too seriously conditioned against all mathematics, who continues through geometry, to solid geometry, analytical geometry, and physics, clerical speed becoming progressively less important, finds these rigorous subjects surprisingly stimulating.

Eighteen midwestern public-high-school pupils tested as shown graphically in figure 15, the entire group high in structural visualization and low in accounting aptitude. Possibly in this instance those encountering school difficulties volunteered for tests, but no evidence suggests such selection elsewhere and the Laboratory sees no reason to suspect it here. While this tested group may not represent the school as a whole, other similar pupils certainly exist, enough to justify a geometry course given before algebra and not requiring the latter subject.

FIGURE 16

ACCOUNTING APTITUDE AND COLLEGE COURSE

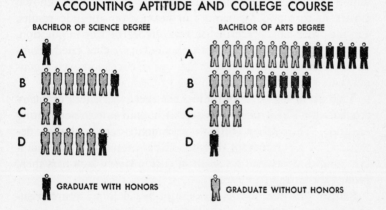

BACHELOR OF SCIENCE DEGREE

BACHELOR OF ARTS DEGREE

A

A

B

B

C

C

D

D

GRADUATE WITH HONORS

GRADUATE WITHOUT HONORS

ONLY ONE MAN WHO GRADED D IN ACCOUNTING APTITUDE, WHEN TESTED EITHER BEFORE COLLEGE OR EARLY IN HIS COURSE, GRADUATED WITH A BACHELOR OF ARTS DEGREE. BUT LOW ACCOUNTING APTITUDE SEEMS NO HANDICAP IN THE BACHELOR OF SCIENCE COURSE.

Figure 16 shows the distribution of accounting aptitude among the same 43 college graduates whose structural visualization is shown in figure 9, page 44. The boy who grades D in accounting aptitude has only a slim chance of gaining an arts degree, a small fraction of that of the boy who grades A. But he has at least an equal chance for a science degree. Based on these findings the Laboratory believes that every boy high in structural visualization and below in accounting aptitude should from the earliest grades have the best possible preparation for a scientific course. This usually involves high-school physics and chemistry, with solid geometry and trigonometry.

No panacea solves the troubles of the boy high in structural visualization and low in accounting aptitude. But the combination is distressing enough to be met in several ways. Geology, archaeology, and anthropology, demand little or no arithmetic and yet use structural visualization. A boy high in the latter should collect in the early grades, before most schools offer such courses, a library dealing with these topics, that he may see their challenge and gain the assurance which comes with mastering any structural field. Occasionally no more than showing a boy clearly a structural goal helps him to overcome the hardships of reaching it. After graduation from high school the remedy becomes extremely difficult, for lack of scientific background frequently drives a boy toward business subjects with no choice in life but unsuitable clerical routine.

48

In a group of high-school juniors the speed of reading a standard passage varies from 150 words a minute to 500. Of the SLOW READING many factors which contribute to slow or inaccurate reading, or to a distaste for books, a few picked at random are probably: low visual discrimination, inaccurate two-eyed coordination, reversal of letters or words, too many fixations, too much time at each, a small vocabulary, and perhaps a difficulty in grouping letters into syllables.

49

Each of the four tests, worksamples 267, 268, 269, and 270, in words, numbers, consonants, and symbols, contains thirty pairs SYLLABLES of comparable items. The words of worksample 267 go more rapidly than numbers; and these in turn faster than consonants. A word probably appears as a single syllable rather than as three separate letters, while a number of similar length, 625, must be read as separate figures. A group of consonants, TZK, unpronounceable as a syllable, takes still longer perhaps because twenty consonants combine in more ways than ten digits, perhaps because certain number combinations, as 25, seem familiar, almost a syllable.

Contingent upon this reasoning the relative speeds of word checking, worksample 267, and consonant checking, worksample 269, should measure the ease with which one groups letters into syllables. If in actual practice the ratio of word-checking to consonant-checking time differs widely for different persons, inability on the part of some to group letters may contribute to reading troubles; and if, as a corollary, the relationship is normal, the cause of reading slowness lies elsewhere.

50

Repetition of a test or of any task does not alter the underlying aptitude, which can be remeasured by another test and found REMEDIAL unchanged, but it develops skill, improves both speed and accuracy of performance. In line with this finding every boy, whether high or low in accounting aptitude, should form the habit of executing each clerical task rapidly in order to repeat it and so gain greater facility.

There lurks in the back of everyone's mind the erroneous assumption that one who hurries makes mistakes. Controlled experiments reveal no statistical evidence to corroborate this fear. One who completes a task from beginning to end under pressure repeats it in measurably shorter time, and still more rapidly on third trial, but the Laboratory finds no mathematical relation between mistakes on first trial and those on second. This suggests that inadvertent errors, which result from speed, do not set the habit of careless inaccuracies. A boy can push himself through a clerical task considerably faster than normal with the assurance that subsequently he repeats it more rapidly, without his careless errors affecting his future performance.

The Laboratory's best measure of concentration is speed, not accuracy. A rare person pushes too strenuously, seeming to overreach himself with abnormal errors, but the devastating tendency is in the reverse direction. For the practical solution of a mathematical problem either in arithmetic, geometry, algebra, or calculus, the Laboratory advances the following rules:

Where structural visualization exceeds accounting aptitude, as with the first five individuals of figure 4, page 10, a boy should lay his pencil aside and analyze his problem from be-

FIGURE 17

WIDE SCATTER OF ACCOUNTING APTITUDE SCORES
WORKSAMPLE 1 WITHIN EACH AGE GROUP

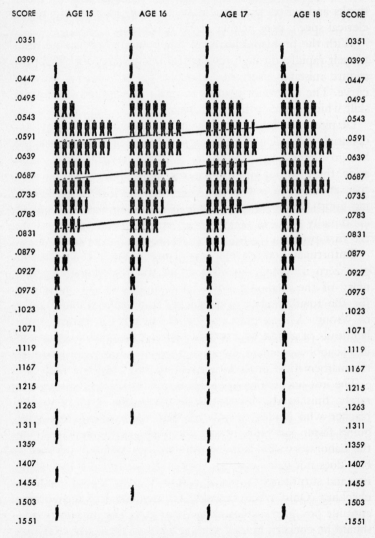

THE THREE THIN NEARLY HORIZONTAL LINES SHOW THE SLIGHT CHANGE WITH AGE OF ACCOUNTING APTITUDE COMPARED WITH THE RANGE WITHIN AN AGE. EACH SYMBOL REPRESENTS 2 PER CENT OF THE BOYS THUS FAR TESTED AT EACH AGE.

ginning to end before entering a single mark on the paper. In many cases speed of thinking depends upon structural visualization; and where this aptitude surpasses accounting aptitude one thinks more rapidly than one records. The boy who thinks and writes simultaneously, slowing his thinking to his clerical speed, does neither at his maximum.

With the problem clearly in mind such a boy should push himself rapidly through the clerical operations. With this procedure mistakes exert no influence on the general learning curve. The important point is to finish rapidly and so gain the skill which comes with completing the task.

Despite his all but overwhelming temptation, the low-accounting-aptitude boy must not stop to check this first example but go directly to the second, again lay his paper and pencil aside, think through the procedure as with the first, and only then perform the operations. One who scores low in accounting aptitude knows that he makes awkward mistakes and so continually starts back over equivocal figures before finishing the first problem.

Unfortunately a few teachers glance at the final answer and give zero if wrong, ignoring either the correctness or ingenuity of the method followed and often awarding no credit for the total number of problems completed whether right or wrong. A single error anywhere in a mathematical problem leads of course to a wrong answer. But the boy's purpose in a school assignment should not be the outcome but learning the mathematical procedures involved and acquiring skill.

The low-accounting-aptitude boy, who interrupts to check, rarely finishes the homework assigned, and even with the teacher who grades on answers only improves his marks by going faster and more nearly completing the assignment; for the Laboratory's evidence shows that by slowing down such a boy does not gain accuracy. His best chance is greater quantity and surprisingly often he reaches a correct result with no checking. Only when through practice the low-accounting-aptitude boy gains sufficient speed to complete his homework, should he concern himself with errors and then only after finishing every assignment. At this point the trained man puts his work aside, starts with fresh paper, and repeats the problem.

The low-accounting-aptitude boy should follow the same procedure. He rarely duplicates the entire lesson, but repetition of no more than the first example gives additional skill.

Finally the Laboratory believes that the low-accounting-aptitude boy belongs in a small school and college where he knows intimately members of the faculty, where he can discuss his own thoughts and not be forced to present them always on paper. One regards the fifteen-year-old boy as less mature than one three years older and education treats him differently. It is no doubt important to teach the tenth-grade boy, whose normal age is fifteen, in a different way from the college freshman, age eighteen. But in accounting aptitude the difference between these two is almost negligible compared with the difference between high and low boys of any one age, so unlike that the Laboratory believes they belong in different schools. Figure 17 shows the wide scatter of individuals. At fifteen one per cent score as low as 0.1551, represented by the half symbol at the lower left of the figure, while another one per cent score as high as 0.0447, at the top of the scoring scale. Compared with this vertical distribution the thin lines running from left to right and rising slightly show change with age.

VIII

CREATIVE IMAGINATION

The phrase CREATIVE IMAGINATION, which labels this aptitude, arouses disparaging remarks, for no one who scores low relishes the thought of lacking originality. The commonest specific criticism centers around the scoring based on total words written in ten minutes, unmindful of spelling, punctuation, or coherence. Most persons contend that a well-constructed, imaginative theme deserves credit, the test's designation demanding the recognition of creativeness. To appreciate the accepted system, based on words, one must pursue the worksample's statistical history to its logical conclusions.

The Fatigue Research Board in London, a government-sponsored group with whom this measuring instrument originated as one of four creative tests, marked the written exercise like any school paper, 1 to 10, judged wholly subjectively by quality of thought. With experience, this stimulating British group reached a personal technique whereby two staff members, grading the same set of papers, arrived at virtually identical results.

To the Human Engineering Laboratory the procedure seemed elusive and not amenable to rigid statistical investigation. After a detailed analysis of two hundred papers, written on the subject: What would happen if all plant life should suddenly disappear from the earth? the Laboratory selected four distinguishable ideas: 1. The immediate catastrophe; 2. Search for a substitute; 3. Probable disappearance of human life; 4. Final aspects of the barren world.

As a four-point scoring scale restricts mathematical freedom, the Laboratory subdivided each of these general headings into some fifty lesser aspects, the immediate catastrophe into riots, rise of prices, government control, and so gained some two hundred scorable points. While satisfactory as compared with the earlier proceeding this proved laborious and inaccurate, for these minor sub-ideas soon overlapped. Ultimately a staff member noticed that each idea, as described by a short phrase in the scoring guide, contained a significant noun: catastrophe, riot, prices; and this led first to scoring on these selected substantives and thence to total number of different nouns.

After grading a hundred papers by this mechanical device the Human Engineering Laboratory asked the English group to rescore them. The results agreed closely. But to illustrate the extraordinarily divergent philosophies which colored aptitude testing from the start the Laboratory staff congratulated itself on finding an automatic system which equaled in accuracy the trained judgment of the English group; they in turn felt that we had wasted two years in arriving at figures no better than their unaided opinion.

Number of nouns used in the ten-minute essay showed a slight relationship (0.20) with the English-vocabulary score, worksample 95. Since the creative-imagination test consists entirely of words, the correlation was not surprising, nor enough to invalidate seriously the results; but the staff aspired to measure the innate creative imagination of undeveloped childhood where, with any relation, lack of vocabulary might interfere.

FIGURE 18

SUGGESTIONS FOR ONE HIGH IN CREATIVE IMAGINATION

					Other Brochures
HIGH CREATIVE IMAGINATION	HIGH STRUCTURAL VISUALIZATION	HIGH INDUCTIVE REASONING	LOW OBSERVATION	SCIENCE TEACHING	AN INDIVIDUAL APPROACH TO SCIENTIFIC PROBLEMS
			HIGH ACCOUNTING APTITUDE	ARCHITECTURE	
		LOW INDUCTIVE REASONING	HIGH PROPORTION APPRAISAL	ARCHITECTURAL SCULPTURE / BOOKBINDING (DESIGN) / DRESS DESIGN / FURNITURE DESIGN / MANUFACTURING DESIGN / STAGE DESIGN / WINDOW DISPLAY	THE TOO-MANY-APTITUDE WOMAN
	LOW STRUCTURAL VISUALIZATION	HIGH INDUCTIVE REASONING	HIGH ANALYTICAL REASONING	CLASSROOM TEACHING / EMPLOYEE TRAINING / FICTION WRITING / HIGH SCHOOL TEACHING / PUBLICITY	UNSOLVED BUSINESS PROBLEMS
		LOW INDUCTIVE REASONING	HIGH PROPORTION APPRAISAL	ART IN ADVERTISING / COMMERCIAL DESIGN / GRAPHIC ARTS / INTERIOR DECORATION	
			PERSONALITY OBJECTIVE	COMMISSION SELLING / INSURANCE SELLING	AN OBJECTIVE APPROACH TO GROUP-INFLUENCING FIELDS

Hoping to reduce the correlation, the research department returned to scoring on number of ideas, the original method abandoned partly because of the labor involved. Instead of lowering the connection with vocabulary, as anticipated, the procedure increased it to 0.30.

The research department next examined unusualness. With two hundred papers it tabulated the frequency of each fancy, one so evident as to occur to most examinees, another unique. Thoughts which appeared regularly drew little credit, rare ones scored higher. This evaluation added further to the correlation with vocabulary (0.40). Another variation, obtained by computing the average unusualness, carried the correlation still higher. Imagination as one normally speaks of it in written themes coincides closely with a wide and exact grasp of English words.

To measure imagination clear of knowledge the staff at this point reversed its direction and scored on total words written in ten minutes. This abolished the relationship with vocabulary and produced a measuring instrument with a reliability of 0.80.

51

Products of imagination, as the world beholds them, spring from an intermingling of two or more aptitudes. New effective mechanical marvels result, not from creative imagination alone, but from this trait steered from the bizarre by structural visualization. Stirring musical compositions come from creative imagination guided by tonal memory. Literature emanates from creative imagination held to a pattern by the two additional traits, inductive reasoning and analytical reasoning. With this in mind the boy who scores high should direct his creative imagination toward activities for which he has other aptitudes to leash the trait; for creative imagination alone frequently leads to an irresponsible bubbling over of ineffectiveness, to a restless turning from the completion of enterprises which demand sustained effort. Perhaps for this reason veteran executives score low in the creative-imagination test, for they cannot afford to be driven daily in some new direction.

CONTROL OF
CREATIVE
IMAGINATION

TABLE VI

CHARACTERISTICS OF DESIGNING ENGINEERS AND INVENTORS

APTITUDE	RATING
STRUCTURAL VISUALIZATION	HIGH
CREATIVE IMAGINATION	HIGH
PERSONALITY	SUBJECTIVE OR EXTREMELY SUBJECTIVE

KNOWLEDGE	RATING
VOCABULARY OF PHYSICS	VERY HIGH
VOCABULARY OF MATHEMATICS	VERY HIGH

52

A manufacturer hired a college graduate, high in structural visualization, objective in personality, but low in creative imagination. Hoping to equip him for an important executive position soon to be open, the organization assigned him a more or less routine job, which consumed no more than half his time but took him to all departments, that he might become acquainted with the factory personnel and gain an intimate knowledge of the product. Six months later the man had picked up no additional duties, assumed no further responsibility, and those in charge agreed that, while he had done his own work well, he lacked what they termed INITIATIVE regarded as indispensable to management. Prompted by the Laboratory, instead of discharging him, they assigned him full-time duties. He fulfilled them not merely satisfactorily but brilliantly, and subsequently received the executive appointment for which he was originally selected and trained. With ability to carry out any supervisory task he saw as vital, he lacked the imagination to create new work.

Many executives possess what the world regards as imagination but score low in the creative-imagination test, worksample 161. The discrepancy is partly a question of terms; for by creative imagination the Laboratory means the trait measured by the test, not all the phrase implies to the general reader.

53

For the boy ambitious to advance scientific knowledge lack of creative imagination may aid by forcing him to build soundly rather than oddly. If high in structural visu-

LOW CREATIVE IMAGINATION

alization he may push forward the advancing frontier of human understanding, reaching entirely unforeseen conclusions, by stepping from the sanctioned to the unknown on careful laboratory experiments. Through high inductive reasoning he may see bold generalizations never before sensed; or through analytical reasoning organize ratified material in wholly original patterns.

54

With creative imagination in excess of other traits a boy must seek some such field as modern advertising, capable of absorbing an incessant flow of novel notions which

HIGH CREATIVE IMAGINATION

other employees put into operation. Or he may find a place in education, see figure 3, page 10, of THE TOO-MANY-APTITUDE WOMAN, and TECHNICAL REPORT 90 for statistical details. One hundred and one high-school and preparatory-school teachers, with an average of ten years' experience, score collectively highest in this characteristic, 71 per cent excelling the median man or woman of similar age. In analytical reasoning and inductive reasoning, traits which guide and control creative imagination, teachers rank next highest; while they score average in accounting aptitude, and low in both structural visualization and observation.

Eighty educational advisors in Civilian Conservation Corps camps also average highest in creative imagination; with the exception of analytical reasoning, which drops to fourth place, the order of all six aptitudes is the same as with high-school teachers.

A boy highest in creative imagination, next highest in the combination of inductive reasoning and analytical reasoning, average in accounting aptitude, and low in both structural visualization and observation, shows the aptitude pattern of the teacher and should conscientiously investigate education.

55

Creative imagination, inductive reasoning, and analytical reasoning, essential traits of the teacher, combined with high

CREATIVE IMAGINATION,
INDUCTIVE REASONING OR
ANALYTICAL REASONING, AND
STRUCTURAL VISUALIZATION

structural visualization, appear among teachers of physics, chemistry, biology, geology, and astronomy. The same pattern suggests occupational therapy as discussed in THE TOO-MANY-APTITUDE WOMAN, vocational training, or industrial employee training.

Aviation needs sympathetic teachers, for in no other field may poor teaching do more harm. A man who has since flown regularly and safely for over twenty years was temporarily and nearly permanently discouraged in the midst of his learning. After steady progress with an appreciative tutor, one lesson with another man, an excellent pilot but poor instructor, made him give up all thought of flying. Except for a chance encounter later with his original teacher aviation would have lost one of its staunch supporters.

Industry is constantly on the alert for born teachers, not only to train recent employees but to retrain skilled workers for new trades. Only lately has the business world begun to picture the potential savings by recording accurately the cost of training: the learner's time when little or nothing is produced, increased inspection, expensive materials wasted and more intangible but greater still customer complaints. All of these can be reduced by skilful training of new workers. Intelligent re-education of old employees can minimize hardships which follow technological advancements.

The designing engineer uses creative imagination but probably not inductive reasoning to the same extent as the teacher. The scientist, seeking general laws, uses inductive reasoning and some creative imagination but scores extremely subjective. The typical writer measures like the teacher, high in creative imagination, inductive reasoning, and analytical reasoning, and every boy with these traits should drive himself to write, force himself to organize his thoughts on paper. But writing as a vocation does not satisfy an extremely objective personality.

56

The General Biological Supply House, 761 East 69th Street, Chicago, Illinois, combines salesmanship and science. Founded in 1914 by Morris Miller Wells, assistant professor of zoology at the University of Chicago, this organization now supplies living specimens, zoological, botanical, and marine; also preserved specimens, demonstration materials, charts, drawings, models, and microscopic slides. Its beautifully illustrated twenty-fifth anniversary catalogue of nearly 750 pages, issued in 1939 and at that time available to schools and colleges, adds to any library.

CREATIVE IMAGINATION, LOW INDUCTIVE REASONING, AND HIGH STRUCTURAL VISUALIZATION

Success in such a business venture probably demands the high structural visualization of the scientist combined with the traits of the salesman: high creative imagination, objectivity, and low inductive reasoning, together with some accounting aptitude. While a boy thus endowed should not compete with a group already supplying the field effectively he might well consider the organization of a somewhat similar enterprise in some other direction.

The General Biological Supply House sells a colony of living ants, together with the queen, from which a boy high in structural visualization may learn more in a few weeks than from a book purchased at approximately the same price. It sells a balanced aquarium to which a boy can add from time to time at little cost a rare fish or a new water plant, simultaneously adding its name to his own vocabulary. Ideally, and especially if high in observation, a boy should own a good scientific microscope, a collection of slides, try his hand both at microphotography and at drawing what he sees, and when possible own even a small telescope.

Almost every boy who scores high in structural visualization, and high in finger or tweezer dexterity, acquires somehow a dilapidated automobile and makes it work. Section 41 of this brochure urges that such a boy collect a library of the sciences. He should in addition have other outlets for his manual energy and his constructive thinking.

57

An objective boy, one who scores other than extremely subjective, high in both structural visualization and creative imagination, should investigate architectural
ARCHITECTURE,   training as an approach to low-cost housing,
HOUSING, AND   slum clearance, and city planning. As early
CITY PLANNING   as age ten he should begin to collect the illustrated architectural books listed in the Laboratory's brochure: THE TOO-MANY-APTITUDE WOMAN. In addition he
should see the following housing developments:

OLD HARBOR VILLAGE, Old Colony Road, South Boston, facing Columbia Park, initiated by Public Works Administration.

MISSION HILL PROJECT, Roxbury, Massachusetts, on Hun-
tington Avenue. For details of Boston housing see a pamphlet:
REHOUSING THE LOW INCOME FAMILIES OF BOSTON, a Review of
the Activities of the Boston Housing Authority, 1936 to 1940.

CHATHAM VILLAGE, Pittsburgh, in the Mount Washington
section, south of the city, a Buhl Foundation enterprise.

HILLSIDE, New York, on the Boston Post Road, a private development owned by Nathan Strauss.

PARKCHESTER, an apartment group in the Bronx in New York,
a Metropolitan Life Insurance Company project.

SUNNYSIDE, Queens, Long Island, New York, near Long Island City, designed by Henry Wright and Clarence Stein.

WILLIAMSBURG, Brooklyn, New York, at the end of the
Williamsburg Bridge.

RADBURN, New Jersey, the Town of the Motor Age, east of
Paterson, also designed by Henry Wright and Clarence Stein.

JULIA C. LATHROP HOMES, Diversey Boulevard, and IDA B.
WELLS HOMES, South Parkway, Chicago, Illinois.

MARIEMONT, 10 miles east of Cincinnati, Ohio.

COLONIAL VILLAGE, Arlington, Virginia, a private enterprise
for white-collar workers, developed by Allie Freed.

GREENBELT, Maryland, between Washington and Baltimore,
7 miles north of the city limits of Washington, just off route 1.

GREENDALE, southwest of Milwaukee, Wisconsin, off route
41 from Chicago.

GREENHILLS, just north of Cincinnati, Ohio.

IX

PROPORTION APPRAISAL

When the McAdory art test proved too complex to yield readily to statistical analysis the Laboratory constructed several apparently simpler tests each of which it hoped would measure one or at least not more than a few of the many factors which seemed present in the original.

Two previous brochures: UNSOLVED BUSINESS PROBLEMS and THE TOO-MANY-APTITUDE WOMAN, discuss the McAdory test and the Laboratory's proportion appraisal test at some length. The first short preliminary form of the latter, worksample 235 form A, showed a surprising and unexpected consistency, for all simple designs, in the proportion chosen as most satisfying. A second and longer form B, worksample 235, with a change in the least attractive of the four proportions from four by one to three by one, and with a reliability of 0.70 (STATISTICAL BULLETIN 774), confirms the earlier findings. Recent data now show the trait growing rapidly from 12 to 19 or 20, where it reaches an adult plateau beyond which it changes no further with age. This type of curve implies an inherent aptitude as distinct from an acquired trait. The next three steps in the research program are:

First, using scores on the adult plateau the research department will correlate proportion appraisal with other aptitudes to determine its independence as a distinct trait. It will check this at one or two separate points on the growth curve, probably ages 16 and 17 where the Laboratory's populations are usually largest.

Second, test administrators will collect more data for women, draw a separate age curve, and so fix the similarities or differences between the sexes. The present age curve is based on males only.

Third, test administrators, more frequently than in the past, will administer both the proportion-appraisal test and the vocabulary of art, worksample 275, to the same person in order that the research department may discover to what extent knowledge of art affects the proportion-appraisal score.

Fourth, if proportion appraisal proves a distinct aptitude, the Laboratory will next correlate the results with the original McAdory art test to study the overlapping and will then try to eliminate proportion appraisal from that earlier and more complex test and so progress toward the remaining factors.

Meanwhile the Laboratory believes that a boy who scores high in the present proportion-appraisal test, worksample 235, should use the trait. If also high in creative imagination, high in structural visualization, and objective in personality, he should investigate architecture, stage design, and possibly furniture design, all discussed in THE TOO-MANY-APTITUDE WOMAN and not rediscussed here, for no brochure can mention all of the literally innumerable fields which exist. While that volume is primarily for women, it lists under five separate headings: architecture, architectural history, community housing, stage design, and furniture design, books which every boy with these traits should know and own.

X

MEMORY FOR DESIGN

Memory for design like proportion appraisal is probably an aptitude although the Laboratory's understanding of the trait still remains far from complete. It is the first characteristic of amateur photographers and the third among those who continue with photography five years or longer. It probably characterizes artists, cartoonists, and art critics. One who scores high in the memory-for-design test, worksample 294, should collect illustrated art books and at least experiment with etching, lithography, sketching, water-colors, or oils.

XI

VOCABULARY OF ART

A high score in either the memory-for-design or proportion-appraisal tests suggests some approach to art, not individual creative work for the objective person, but architecture, museum management, fine printing, or perhaps commercial design, fields where success depends as much on a knowledge of art as upon inherent gifts.

One attracted by furniture design and construction should own:

ENCYCLOPEDIA OF FURNITURE by Joseph Aronson, illustrated with 1115 photographs; Crown Publishers, 1940.

ENGLISH FURNITURE FROM GOTHIC TO SHERATON by Herbert Cescinsky; Garden City Publishing Company, 1937, in addition to the books listed in THE TOO-MANY-APTITUDE WOMAN.

XII

KNOWLEDGE OF PAINTINGS

The knowledge-of-paintings test, worksample 183, despite its name, may measure not such pure knowledge as do the various vocabulary tests. Observation for example probably aids in remembering paintings more than in gaining a vocabulary; and for this reason the Laboratory urges the boy who scores high in observation to use this aptitude in learning through pictures. One who scores high in the knowledge-of-paintings test almost automatically absorbs a knowledge of architectural styles, of art history, and ultimately of history itself, often more easily than through the printed page.

XIII

INDUCTIVE REASONING

Each item of the inductive-reasoning test contains pictures of six familiar objects, from which one picks rapidly, under pressure, three of the same sort, of the same type or class. The earliest version had eight pictures to the line, four of one type, and correlated with accounting aptitude. Reduction to the present six per line the research department hoped would eliminate the overlapping. But the change had no effect; the speed with which one succeeds in the present test, worksample 164, still correlates (0.24) with accounting aptitude.

TABLE VII

PATTERN OF APTITUDES AND KNOWLEDGE BELIEVED TO
DISTINGUISH RESEARCH SCIENTISTS

APTITUDE	RATING
STRUCTURAL VISUALIZATION	HIGH
INDUCTIVE REASONING	HIGH
PERSONALITY	SUBJECTIVE OR EXTREMELY SUBJECTIVE

KNOWLEDGE	RATING
VOCABULARY OF PHYSICS	VERY HIGH
VOCABULARY OF MATHEMATICS	VERY HIGH

Rapidity in completing the inductive-reasoning test proves the second outstanding characteristic of 101 high-school and preparatory-school teachers with an average of nine and a half years' experience. In the learning process a boy acquires permanently only words near the border of his English vocabulary at the time. This seems to imply that he must tie the unknown term to his present knowledge before it becomes a part of his permanent store. A successful teacher may be one who recognizes relationships, common factors; and fast time in the inductive-reasoning test may show this gift. Whatever the test measures, it indicates without question a characteristic of men and women who continue in teaching.

58

While teachers especially of English, history, and the languages, score low in structural visualization those in mathematics and the sciences average high. See figure 17, page 99, of THE TOO-MANY-APTITUDE WOMAN, for comparative distributions of structural-visualization scores among teachers of language and of the sciences. See also figure 3, page 10, of the same book for the distribution by letter grades of five traits among established teachers in general.

STRUCTURAL VISUALIZATION AND TEACHING

XIV

ANALYTICAL REASONING

The analytical-reasoning test, invented by Samuel Horton in 1937, has not yet been freed from disturbing factors. It still correlates 0.38 with structural visualization, 0.27 with observation, and 0.24 with tweezer dexterity. While these figures apply to adults, for whom intercorrelations are usually slightly higher than for intermediates, analytical reasoning as now measured is not a completely independent trait. For comparison, the newest accounting-aptitude test, worksample 268, correlates only 0.09 with structural visualization, 0.10 with observation, and 0.14 with tweezer dexterity, based on intermediates, figures which approach the ideal zero. This independence is however the result of twenty years' work.

For practical purposes, a high score in the analytical-reasoning test indicates a trait which should be used, probably a gift for organizing material, for the mental process followed by an author in coordinating his ideas or by a scientist in formulating a research program. Every boy or girl high in this trait should read the chapters on Carl Linnaeus in GREEN LAURELS by Donald Culross Peattie, Garden City Publishing Company, 1938, for it may have been some such trait which inspired the Linnaean system.

While accounting aptitude characterizes both the accurate bookkeeper and the certified public accountant, high analytical reasoning distinguishes the latter. It probably embodies his superior insight for organization of heterogeneous entries.

Validation studies show analytical reasoning, as now measured, to be in order of importance the third characteristic of teachers. It is perhaps an aptitude for assembling and arranging the materials of a course. The combination, creative imagination, inductive reasoning, and analytical reasoning, especially in this order, suggests high-school, preparatory-school, or college teaching; or, for one not attracted by the classroom, more informal training in industry, in manufacturing, or in farm extension as discussed on page 65, which probably uses these same teaching traits coupled with structural visualization.

XV

JUDGMENT

The question: Can the Laboratory measure JUDGMENT? recurs in every discussion of aptitudes. Is any such trait mathematically separable from others; or is it a compound; or not an inherent aptitude at all but instead the outcome of wide experience? In the previous brochure: THE TOO-MANY-APTITUDE WOMAN, the research department reported its complete failure to measure judgment after two years' work, despite a grant from the Genradco Trust for this express purpose. Now new findings give hope of ultimate success.

An early step in the act of judgment is assembling the pertinent facts at one's command; then comes fitting them together and arriving at an answer which later proves near enough the truth to have been a serviceable guide to one's actions. At the suggestion of Melville Eastham, the Laboratory designed worksample 276. This test asks a series of such apparently unanswerable questions as: How many tons of steel were used in building New York City?, questions to which, by the laws of chance, an insignificant percentage of examinees know the direct answers; but which the average man can approximate by fitting together bits of information at his disposal.

When the staff first administered worksample 276 few persons came to the right conclusion and the test seemed worthless. Based on the percentage of right answers to each of the twelve questions, even though these seemed little more than luck, the Laboratory rearranged the items in order of difficulty, starting with the easiest. When the original test began with a difficult item many persons got the erroneous impression that they could arrive at an answer only by pure guess and so continued with this set, never realizing they might approach the truth by reasoning. In the rearranged test almost everyone approximates an answer to the first question and so starts with the predicate that he can reach the correct answer to items which before seemed quite impossible. With this new arrangement the accuracy of the test, which before equaled zero, is now sufficiently high to give an excellent basis for further analysis.

Some items, which call on specialized knowledge possessed by a significant percentage of examinees and not by others, must be changed to bring them within the informational compass of all. Other items seem to require a gift for estimating sizes, lengths, or weights. Reaching a shrewd estimate in these cases may be judgment; and Samuel Reed has designed worksample 302 with the hope ultimately of measuring this mental process separately from still a third which seems to enter judgment, an intellectual gift for deducing a right conclusion directly from accepted facts.

This last step in the judgment process the Laboratory now tries to measure directly by means of worksample 277. Each item of this test states a conclusion. The problem is to pick, from four given facts, the pair from which the conclusion follows. The test as now designed is difficult. Statistically one person in six should pick the correct two out of four by luck. In actual practice an unselected group of examinees pick the correct two approximately half the time. While far from conclusive the results of this test suggest that one of the difficult steps in the judgment process is reaching a correct conclusion from known statements.

How much the study of formal logic affects this reasoning and how much some inherent aptitude determines the outcome is another of the many unanswered questions on which the Laboratory's experiments must some day throw light.

XVI

DEDUCTIVE REASONING

In attempting to isolate DEDUCTIVE REASONING from INDUCTIVE, as now measured by worksample 164, Samuel Horton devised worksample 248. Approached from another point of view and, as shown by the worksample number, prior to the judgment study, this test seems so similar to worksample 277 as possibly to measure the same trait. Because the battery committee hesitates to administer two such similar experimental tests to the same person the research department has as yet no data from which to compute a correlation based on empirical results.

XVII

OBSERVATION

In the observation test the examinee studies for one minute an eight by ten photograph of some twenty familiar objects. Laying this aside, he takes another differing in one or more ways from the original. The speed and accuracy with which he names the changes determine his score. An early form, worksample 184, where the designer piled articles on top of one another, a thin box of cigarettes on a small rectangular book, and a watch above, correlated 0.32 to 0.47 with structural visualization as indicated by the black cube, worksample 167, and 0.32 with the same trait as shown by the wiggly block. The dependence of one test on another and the effect of slight changes in each give unexpected insight into the characteristics measured; examinees low in structural visualization failed to realize the removal of the cigarette box from under the watch, failed also to notice the turning upside down of any article. The revised observation test, worksample 206, which displays nothing resting on anything else and nothing turned over, correlates less than the original figure, only 0.26, with structural visualization.

Incredible as it may seem, any object turned over or resting on another presents a serious mental obstacle to one who scores low in structural visualization. In the design of each non-structural test the psychometrician must spread his objects, never allowing them to overlap or turn upside down. The boy low in structural visualization must avoid occupations in which such phenomena occur, probably all fields in which material objects play a substantial part, as architecture and engineering. This agrees with the finding that men and women low in the characteristic succeed in writing, banking, editorial work, advertising, law, and teaching, not one of which deals primarily with the handling of concrete materials.

Paralleling its reduction of the structural element in the observation test the research department attacked the problem of eliminating observation from its structural tests. With the original black cube, then called worksample 167, the administrator proffered the twenty-seven blocks correctly assembled, then took them apart, and asked the examinee to reassemble as before. This procedure produced a significant relation between black-cube scores and the observation test, correlation 0.41-0.47, TECHNICAL REPORT 52, examinees high in observation gaining enough by inspecting the complete structure to have a measurable advantage. Now the administrator describes the solid to be built but does not expose it in advance. The results, called worksample 210 and, in the still newer form, worksamples 245 and 246, correlate zero (0.05-0.06) with observation.

Every boy, high in observation, should turn the trait to advantage by seeing for himself. He frequently gains more lasting knowledge from a museum hour than from worrying facts from some cumbrous tome. He should collect illustrated books and pamphlets, colored charts and schematic diagrams, own a motion-picture projector and rent or accumulate films, building his reading about his gift for exact observation.

59

From the fact that everyone learns English words in the same order follows the conclusion that each new acquisition depends on the knowledge of some word previously acquired; the greatest single block to further advance is lack of background on which to build. But as a first word must originally have been learned directly from an action or an object, and not from another word, a boy high in observation can learn many in like manner, and with each acquisition come, with little additional effort, hosts of others dependent upon it.

OBSERVATION AND VOCABULARY

The gifted teacher or rare headmaster carries in mind the scholastic idiosyncrasies of numerous students; but effective encouragement of museum visits depends primarily on parents. With the present diversity in every classroom, with talented pupils high in structural visualization who should learn through laboratory experiments, with others high in tonal memory who should be encouraged in music, with others high in number memory, with still others high in accounting aptitude, and only a few with observation as their outstanding trait, no teacher can encourage to the full each unusual combination of traits.

A parent can do more. A father can conveniently drop his son at a museum entrance Saturday morning, or a mother leave him there while she shops. A father with sufficient money should have his son's entire school class tested until he finds a companion for these museum visits equally high in observation. The annual trip made by many schools is not enough for selected pupils who score high.

Not until a boy high in observation visits the museums in his locality regularly once a week for a year and knows both the English and the Latin name of every animal, bird, plant, fish, and the various races of man, has he a right to lament over the hardships of school work. Geography becomes more alive when he pictures primitive inhabitants and indigenous animals, history more colorful if he knows the authentic costumes worn at each era, English composition more alluring as he accumulates first-hand observations about which to write.

60

A Chicago boy high in observation should know: WHAT TO SEE AND DO IN CHICAGO, published by the Chicago Association of Commerce, price ten cents. A boy high in observation, who lives near Boston, New York, or Philadelphia, should catalogue for himself the science, art, natural history, and industrial museums within reach, tabulate their departments, collect their catalogues, and learn to know each intimately.

CHICAGO MUSEUMS

The Field Museum of Natural History in Grant Park in Chicago, open 9 A.M. to 4 P.M. in the winter, 9 A.M. to 6 P.M. in the summer, and always free to children, has four major departments: anthropology, botany, geology, and zoology. From this last department a boy should add weekly to his own library one of its leaflets:

THE WHITE-TAILED DEER	10 cents
CHICAGO WINTER BIRDS	10 cents
THE AMERICAN ALLIGATOR	10 cents
THE PERIODICAL CICADA	10 cents
THE MAN-EATING LIONS OF TSAVO	50 cents

Parents should encourage the collection of such pamphlets issued by museums describing the objects seen so that a boy's reading applies directly to his visits, and then add the related books recommended; even though a boy may not seem to read, he absorbs knowledge in a different channel from the more scholastically-minded person.

Museum of Science and Industry in Jackson Park, at Fifty-seventh Street and Lake Michigan, covers physics, chemistry, geology, mining, agriculture, medicine, dentistry, pharmacy, power, transportation, civil engineering, and the graphic arts, also an operating coal mine, a foundry, and a miniature railroad.

Chicago Academy of Sciences, Lincoln Park, 2001 North Clark Street, shows birds, mammals, insects, minerals, and fossils.

The boy eager to glean a bit more knowledge from the printed page should own on his own shelves in his own room:

THE INSECT BOOK by Leland O. Howard; Doubleday, Page & Company, 1910.

THE BUTTERFLY BOOK by W. J. Holland; Doubleday, Page & Company, 1914.

THE OUTLINE OF NATURAL HISTORY by Sir J. Arthur Thomson; Putnam's, 1931, a delightfully written nature study.

SNAKES OF THE WORLD by Raymond L. Ditmars; Macmillan, 1941.

REPTILES OF THE WORLD by Raymond L. Ditmars; Macmillan, 1933. This book describes countless species of crocodiles, lizards, snakes, and turtles. It cannot be read from beginning to end but should wait on a boy's shelf ready for reference.

61

In a manufacturing organization an objective boy, high in observation and above average in structural visualization, may gain a supervisory position by way of the inspection department. See UNSOLVED BUSINESS PROBLEMS. In science, and especially for the extremely subjective boy, high observation suggests work with the microscope: anatomy, bacteriology, or metallography; or work with the telescope in astronomy. See THE TOO-MANY-APTITUDE WOMAN.

STRUCTURAL VISUALIZATION AND OBSERVATION

62

The presence of observation always suggests to the author some activity in the fine arts, although little direct statistical evidence as yet confirms this feeling. Ob-

OBSERVATION, CREATIVE
IMAGINATION, AND
STRUCTURAL VISUALIZATION

servation combined with proportion appraisal, memory for design, or creative imagination, strengthens the belief that a boy should try expressing himself through sketching or painting. These traits combined with structural visualization suggest sculpture. A set of wood-carving tools is not prohibitive in cost and even though a boy neglects them at first he surprisingly often picks them up later, especially if he has with them books on the techniques, history, and styles, of wood carving. A boy with this combination of aptitudes should also own clay, plasticine, and books on sculpture and on casting with both plaster of Paris and bronze.

XVIII

NUMBER MEMORY

Examinees who score low in the number-memory test, work-sample 165, sit on the edge of the chair in taking the test, grow progressively more nervous as they miss numbers, and exhibit the symptoms of extreme nervous pressure. Others, who score high, sit back quietly, relaxed, absorbing and storing away in their minds one exposed number after another.

An industrialist, seeking an executive for his production planning department, asked the Laboratory to locate a man capable of working under constant tension, for in such work the telephone rings incessantly, orders arrive and must be promised, if put off too long they may be lost, foremen call from the factory that some essential item has not arrived, a promise cannot be met. The effectual solution to this industrial problem is not a phlegmatic man capable of withstanding the nervous strain of working under continual external pressure, but instead a man who scores high enough in number memory to juggle perpetual orders easily and well without undue exertion.

In applying for industrial work a boy who rates high in number memory should consider asking specifically for production planning or control, sometimes called expediting, chasing, or production following. The work takes one ordinarily to every department, forces one to learn every operation, and gives intimate and extensive knowledge of a factory and of a product.

XIX

TONAL MEMORY

Prior to the accumulation of measured data, speculative considerations predicted that tonal memory might prove the illusive aptitude which helps some boys to pick up foreign languages and retain the sounds of strange English words heard over the radio and in family conversation. But confirmed tabulations disclose no mathematical connection between measured English vocabulary, worksample 95, and tonal memory, worksample 215, retention of the musical tunes of three, four, five, and six notes played from the phonograph record. Either the mnemonic gift for carrying sounds in mind takes no important role in collecting words; or tonal memory, as measured by the test, differs from general aural memory. The last seems true, for statistical analyses already place at least two separate types of visual memory, and suggest others, and will isolate in due time probably as many varieties of aural memory.

63

Pitch discrimination, another aural trait separate from tonal memory, enables its possessors to distinguish two audible vibration frequencies, emitted electrically one after the other and differing slightly in pitch. Dependent no doubt on the internal structure of the physical ear, the gift enters the performance of stringed musical instruments without frets, listed in detail in figure 13, page 88, of the Laboratory's brochure: THE TOO-MANY-APTITUDE WOMAN, more than of keyboard instruments, such as the piano and organ, figure 14, page 90, of the same brochure.

PITCH DISCRIMINATION

64

High in the compilation tonal memory and structural visualization, an engineering graduate works on the mechanical design
of musical instruments to reproduce more
TONAL MEMORY
faithfully over the radio. The modern piano
AND STRUCTURAL
originated with an inventive genius little
VISUALIZATION
more than two hundred years ago; while
the harpsichord, the clavichord, and the spinet, developed from
cruder forebears. Still more refined forms, embodying the
technical developments of the twentieth century, will inevitably
appear in the coming years.

A manufacturing executive, with tonal memory, pitch discrimination, and structural visualization, produces radio sets
of exceptional quality. An objective college graduate, with the
same traits, now uses his objectivity as executive head of his
own department, after achieving an enviable reputation by
setting up loud speakers and amplifying devices for special oc-
casions, where he doubtless used tonal memory and pitch discrimination in gaining sound quality, and certainly taxed his
structural visualization by solving the acoustical and installation problems in a score of convention halls. Another, tested
by the Laboratory and similarly high in tonal memory, in-
stalled the loud speakers for two national, political conventions
and for an important Pan-American conference. Somewhere,
common to the varied activities of these several men, are the
gifts called tonal memory and pitch discrimination, measured
by worksamples 215 and 315.

Perhaps the entire field of acoustical engineering demands
either tonal memory or pitch discrimination or both. Radio
manufacturers, the Ediphone and Dictaphone corporations producing sound recorders for dictating letters and instructions at
one's own convenience, in the early morning, in the evening, on
Sundays or holidays, on the way home at night in one's own
automobile, or in one's office without interrupting a secretary
or stenographer, and other organizations manufacturing mechanical apparatus for recording speeches to be filed or released
later in printed form, all seek electrical, mechanical, and acoustical engineers; for the design, fabrication, and installation, of

diverse sound-producing apparatus as telephones, carillons, organs, and the transmitting and receiving boxes into which business executives speak to associates, illustrate tasks which no doubt demand a combination of structural visualization, and either tonal memory or pitch discrimination.

To a father whose son grades high not only in tonal memory and structural visualization, but also in creative imagination and inductive reasoning, the Laboratory suggested a combination of engineering and music, together with training in writing, of incalculable value in every position. The father, conceiving himself as highly practical, brushed music aside as out of the question, impractical, visionary, and stated truthfully that only the exception earns a living at writing. This left engineering, which he wished his son to pursue. The test administrator, in despair at his own ineffectiveness in expressing his point of view, finally asked: 'Is there any one engineer you would like your son to resemble? ' and the father unhesitantly named an authority in sound transmission, author of an accepted book on the subject, a man whose success embraces writing, a study of sound, and engineering, exactly the synthesis the Laboratory recommended. Suddenly this father realized that his ideal for his son involved not merely engineering; for no boy succeeds today in engineering alone, but always in some branch, some phase, some aspect of the subject.

Much satisfaction comes from excelling at one's job; and yet the engineer who relies exclusively on structural visualization and makes no effort to use any other trait does his work no better than probably one man in every two under similar circumstances, for if one believes the latest evidence then each man possesses structural visualization to the full or lacks it wholly. One's only chance of more than ordinary excellence is not more structural visualization but using a larger number of different aptitudes.

One boy in two grades above average, above the median, in structural visualization, one in four above the median in two aptitudes, one in eight above in three, one in sixteen above in four. The larger the number of aptitudes a boy combines the more unusual the place he makes. Yet most parents insist upon discussing some such stereotyped job as ENGINEERING.

FIGURE 19

CONTINUED STUDY OF THE PIANO DEMANDS
HIGH ACCOUNTING APTITUDE

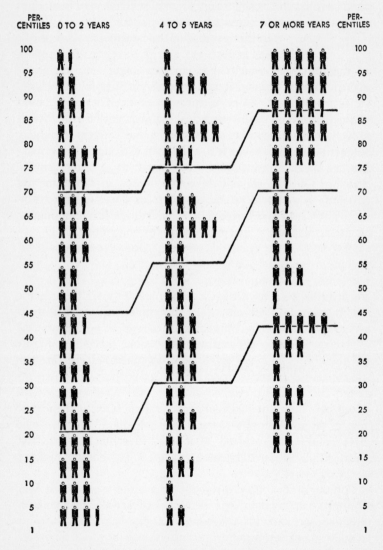

BOYS WHO SCORE LOW IN ACCOUNTING APTITUDE BECOME DISCOURAGED WITH ANY
INSTRUMENT SUCH AS THE PIANO FOR WHICH SCORES APPEAR ON TWO STAVES.

65

Cumulative evidence suggests that tonal memory, like structural visualization, when finally isolated will not vary in amount but instead be either present in full or absent.

MUSICAL PERFORMANCE

On this assumption an exceptional score in the present test, worksample 215, shows no more of the trait than a score considerably lower but still above average; and in consequence does not alone justify trying music as a profession. To perform on the concert stage one must ordinarily possess tonal memory, but in addition other traits as well, at least pitch discrimination together with the extremely subjective personality of the performer, the combination making one succeed rather than the quantity of any one element. The boy who scores objective in personality, to whom this brochure is directed, in any of the three divisions called subjective, objective, or extremely objective, is not in the opinion of the staff happy in the life of a performing artist.

66

For many years it has seemed to members of the staff that music for the piano, written on two staves which must be read simultaneously, demands more accounting

ACCOUNTING APTITUDE AND THE PIANO

aptitude than does the violin. Figure 19 shows the distribution of this characteristic among a large group who at the time they were tested had studied the piano less than two years. Some of the group will continue but many of them had already abandoned music. At the center appears the distribution of those who have continued the piano more than four but less than five years; while at the right are those who have continued seven years or more.

Although the chart gives the impression that those who continue gain accounting aptitude, considerable evidence from other sources shows that those low in the characteristic do not acquire it but instead drop the piano, leaving those who continue a selected group who originally scored high in accounting aptitude. Boys high in tonal memory but low in accounting aptitude should avoid the piano and similar instruments for which scores appear on two staves, turning instead to instruments clerically less complicated. Boys already forced by purblind tradition to hours at the keyboard should not allow a distaste for its clerical barrier to turn them from all music.

67

As already recorded, figure 11, page 53, in a group who studied the violin for one year or less, and in a majority of cases dropped music or shifted to another instrument, no one ranks *A* in finger dexterity, while an overwhelming proportion grade below average, *C* or *D*. Among those who persist with the violin more than one but at the time of the test less than four years, finger dexterity seems, except for chance differences, evenly distributed. But a clear majority of those who continue beyond this point, with an average of five and a half years at the violin, rank above average.

FINGER DEXTERITY
AND THE VIOLIN

As with accounting aptitude and the piano, two interpretations superficially fit the facts: either those who persist with the violin acquire finger dexterity; or they originally possessed this needed trait. Evidence from other sources shows finger dexterity to be an aptitude and the second of these two alternatives to play the larger part. Were the first true then something makes some boys continue with the violin and others stop. This may be a trait, not yet measured, called vaguely persistence. If persistence is independent of finger dexterity then those who lack persistence and who start and stop the violin should be unselected for finger dexterity. But the distribution curve at the left of figure 11 shows those who start and stop the violin clearly low in finger dexterity.

One can of course argue that those who score low in finger dexterity and yet continue the violin need more persistence than those who start high in finger dexterity. But this is equivalent to saying that a boy who scores low in finger dexterity has less chance of continuing with the violin than one who scores high and if interested in music should probably start with some other phase requiring less of this type of dexterity.

Not strictly so three-dimensional as a steel building or suspension bridge, an intricate musical composition seems nevertheless to tax the trait measured by the wiggly block; so that high structural visualization, together with tonal memory and perhaps creative imagination, suggest composing. Certainly a boy with this group of traits should take a course in harmony, read on the subject, and try composing.

68

For one who scores objective in personality, such major business enterprises as radio, motion pictures, and the theater, operate with a background of music. In this

TONAL MEMORY
AND OBJECTIVITY

general direction one who excels in tonal memory and becomes a mechanic, engineer, clerk, production follower, minor executive, or even an office boy, finds congenial working companions and stumbles on more ways of using the trait than in a bank, insurance company, or airplane factory.

The often present but unexpressed feeling that one should reserve tonal memory for a hobby to be thoroughly savored and not contaminated by commercial profit implies that one does not expect to enjoy work. But an engineer, a draftsman, or a mechanic, with some organization whose product involves sound, may enjoy music evenings as much as one who works for a steel mill; and there is always the off chance that he may find in his work an enjoyable use for the trait. As a man uses more nearly his total ability, satisfaction with work increases until he may get the same full pleasure as from a hobby.

xx

VOCABULARY OF MUSIC

Frequently a conscientious musician declares that he seems to go about so far in his profession, or more often in the study of some special composition, and then seems blocked, unable to go further regardless of work. One of the purposes of accurate tests is to aid such a person to isolate and recognize the exact

barrier holding him back. It may be lack of some vital aptitude. Far more often it is lack of acquirable knowledge. Although one thinks of the fine arts as depending on divine in-
spiration, the Laboratory is constantly surprised by the remarkably high knowledge scores made by distinguished artists.

XXI

GENERAL INTELLIGENCE

Out of the inveterate conviction that flying machines weighing tons were ridiculous impracticalities has materialized, within
the easy memories of persons still alive, the modern commercial plane carrying its score or more of passengers in excess
of two hundred miles an hour. Expressed in speed, a business
man now travels in sixty minutes a distance which a few years
past took five hours by fast train and thirty, forty, or fifty, by
stage coach a century and a half ago. No one with a serious
purpose in mind would return permanently to coaching days.
But some, given opportunity to study with Plato, would en-
thusiastically go back many centuries, for education has pro-
gressed noticeably slower than mechanical devices.

In the belief that basic to safe flying, to rapid communication, to the telephone, the radio, and television, lie advancements in pure science, in the art of measuring, in the isolation
of the chemical elements, in the microscopic study of alloys,
the Human Engineering Laboratory has set itself the task of
pushing forward a bit the pure science of human behavior.
Can man's acts be measured as can electric currents, can his
manners of thinking be isolated and studied separately as can
the chemical elements, independent of disturbing factors?

Tacitly accepting the vital importance of the much-discussed
general intelligence, the Human Engineering Laboratory began, two decades ago, by administering a general test to a group
of business executives. As expected, they scored high, a manifestly INTELLIGENT group.

Subsequently, in discussing the results, an experienced factory foreman declared that while he saw the need of general
intelligence among the executive group, he sought in his own

operators a more specific facility, finger dexterity, for the assembly of small parts. At his instigation, the Laboratory arrived at its finger-dexterity test, worksample 16, scored on the time required to pick up 300 metal pins and to place them three at a time in 100 drilled holes. Speed of performance, important in specialized operations, shows no statistical connection with the general-intelligence score of the same person.

Developed at the insistence of a General Electric forewoman, worksample 18, now said to measure tweezer dexterity, proves equally independent of general intelligence and unexpectedly independent of finger dexterity. In placing an untrained employee in the industrial world, high finger dexterity suggests small assembly operations, tweezer dexterity suggests watchmaking or miniature-instrument work, and general intelligence remains an untapped reservoir from which innumerable traits may in time be drawn.

Tonal memory as now measured by worksample 215, observation as measured by worksample 206, and personality, worksample 35, were accepted as presumably independent of intelligence, and all three prove so statistically.

Armchair speculators, who discussed the problem in advance, disagreed as to whether structural visualization, when measured, would prove an intellectual function or be independent of general intelligence. Statistics confirm the last, for this trait, measured by worksample 5, correlates zero with general-intelligence scores. Tabulations also prove its independence of finger dexterity, of tweezer dexterity, of tonal memory, of personality, and its virtual independence of observation although a slight correlation still exists as discussed in part xvii. Thus step by step laboratory measurements submitted to mathematical analysis uncover traits outside the scope of GENERAL INTELLIGENCE.

To predict school performance implies a scholastic test which contains in their proper proportions the intellectual elements affecting specifically academic accomplishment. But to predict success or failure in other directions demands not only the isolation of various types of manual dexterity entering factory operations, but in addition a set of measuring instruments helpful in analyzing any social, industrial, or educational situation involving human decisions and courses of action.

FIGURE 20

ENGLISH VOCABULARY IMPROVES WITH AGE

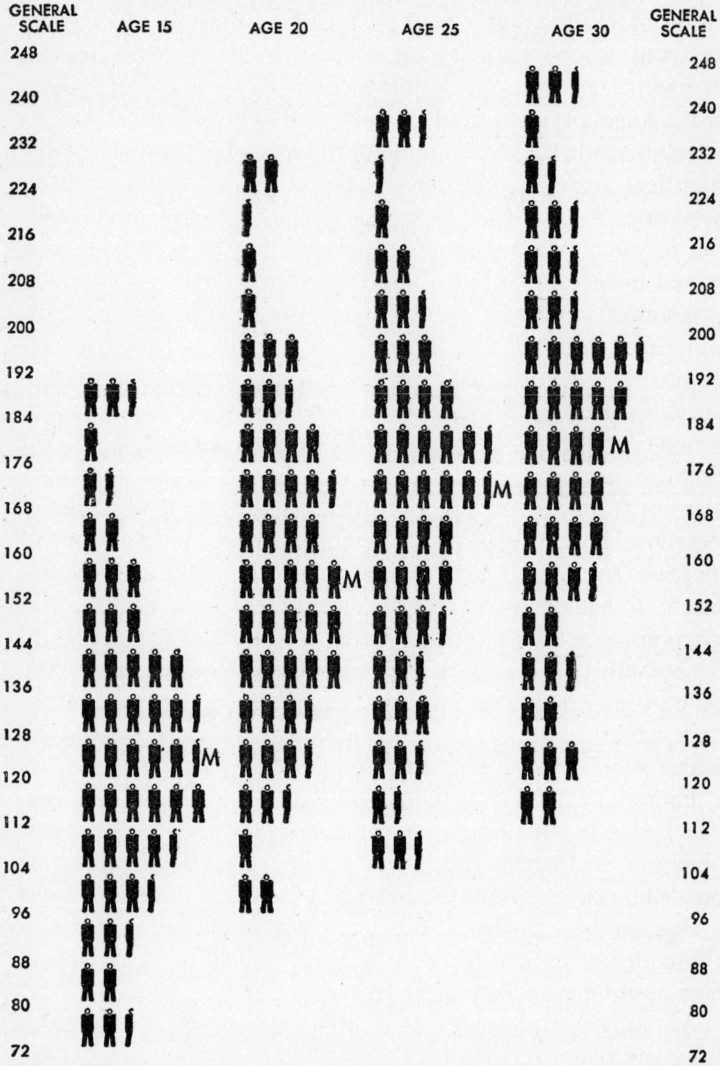

EACH SYMBOL REPRESENTS 2 PER CENT OF THE MALES OF EACH AGE SHOWN AT THE TOP. M LOCATES THE MEDIAN OR CENTER PERSON. NOTICE THAT AS YOUNG AS FIFTEEN, 5 PER CENT OF BOYS SCORE ABOVE THE AVERAGE MAN AGE THIRTY; WHILE AT THIS LAST AGE 4 PER CENT STILL SCORE BELOW THE AVERAGE FIFTEEN-YEAR-OLD BOY.

The first attempt to separate general intelligence itself into its parts resulted in worksample 1. This test resembled an actual page in several general tests. Worksample 268, the latest revision of worksample 1, and now said to measure ACCOUNTING APTITUDE, shows an accuracy of 0.92, and yet correlates less than 0.10 with the remaining sections of general-intelligence tests. Accounting aptitude grows with chronological age to an adult maturity. Accounting-aptitude scores show all of the statistical features which the Laboratory associates with an APTITUDE. A boy who lacks this part of general intelligence can to some extent meet the deficiency by the techniques discussed in section 50 but cannot acquire the trait.

Another significant part of many general-intelligence tests, and particularly of the Binet-Simon test in the Stanford revision, is the vocabulary section. The Laboratory's English vocabulary test, worksample 95, correlates (0.60 to 0.85) with general intelligence as measured by various standard tests. Yet English-vocabulary scores differ radically in statistical characteristics from accounting aptitude. They improve with schooling more directly than with chronological age, and continue to increase through life, never attaining an adult plateau. See figure 20 which shows vocabulary distributions, at five year intervals, in terms of the general scale. One who scores low on the vocabulary section of a general-intelligence test can at any time of life commit to memory the meanings of words and so concurrently improve his score in all general-intelligence tests which require word definitions.

Financial success, earnings, position, especially in later life, check closely with English vocabulary. To the boy who scores objective an English vocabulary seems particularly important; one who scores below the average of college graduates lacks a characteristic possessed by successful executives and has in consequence less chance of using his personality in an important position especially after forty.

An industrial promoter some fifty years of age, tested carefully and sent a report of his scores, felt that what he regarded as his own extraordinary personal history warranted more consideration than either the test administrator or report writer had seemed to accord it and requested a special appointment to discuss his problems. He scored brilliantly high in structural visualization, high in accounting aptitude, and objective in personality, but only C in English vocabulary. Judged by his test scores alone he should have succeeded to the age of forty. At about this point vocabulary becomes gradually more important than aptitudes, and the man could expect no further advance, might even fail to hold a position already achieved .

Exactly this happened. The man gained a national reputation for solving difficult problems, for meeting unusual situations. He earned large fees but always just failed to gain the major executive title he thought he deserved. To the age of forty he was happy attacking one apparently insolvable problem after another. Between forty and forty-five he turned gradually dissatisfied with his accomplishments, felt he should make a permanent place. At fifty, entirely unknown to a business world which had forgotten his former successes, he held a minor salary job largely through a considerate friend.

Bafflingly inexplicable to him, his story supplied only the details of a meteoric life the Laboratory could have predicted thirty years earlier. While one whose vocabulary exceeds his aptitudes achieves a place for himself commensurate with the former, advancing progressively through life, another, whose vocabulary remains below his aptitudes, finds the latter beginning to fail him at about age forty and often drops back to the level of his lesser vocabulary, either losing his job or seeing younger men stride past him.

In most contexts the word SUCCESS conveys no exact notion. At one time it implies commercial earnings, at another advancement in title or position, at a third an idealistic contribution to the future, leaving the world richer for one's efforts. The first two, susceptible to exact statistical study, both check closely with English vocabulary.

The chairman of a New York corporation knew of six vice-presidential openings. Under him were ten men of his own careful choosing and hired originally with just such opportunities in mind. Yet when the time arrived he did not actually promote one, although passing them over meant that because of age they would probably have no second chance. Tested at this point by the Human Engineering Laboratory, all showed

exactly the aptitudes for major executive work and had clearly
been chosen initially with remarkable insight. But without
exception they scored below the twentieth percentile in vocabulary. Two of the men, with the rare distinction of scoring
at the 100th percentile in the aptitudes required for their own
jobs, scored one at the fifth percentile in vocabulary, the
other at the third. Not one of the ten became an officer.
The six men promoted to vice presidencies and then tested
scored measurably below the others in inherent ability but
without exception above the eightieth percentile in vocabulary.
One who sees this happen time and again over a span of years
gains an esteem for vocabulary difficult to exaggerate and
almost impossible to convey to the boy high in aptitudes.

In discussing the situation with the men passed over they
declared they had done their own jobs well and argued that
more vocabulary would not have helped them, and that if advanced they would get more vocabulary on the new job, which
is probably not true for vocabulary does not come easily. They
felt they knew enough words to express themselves simply.
Why then know EXEGESIS, ANIMADVERSION, and BUCCAL, which
never occur in conversation? The Laboratory has no answer
except the facts, based on statistical findings, which it attempts
to state. Although the staff may become so much engrossed in
some individual that it oversteps the bounds and urges too
vehemently its own point of view, it aims at least in theory to
present its findings deferentially and to go no further.

69

To parents, ambitious to do everything in their power to help
the low-vocabulary boy, the Laboratory recommends six specific steps. First: Parents should furnish every boy
BUILDING   a regular allowance for books in his own field of
A LIBRARY   interest, books for his own shelves, not for the
family library. A boy may score discouragingly low in general English vocabulary and simultaneously at the top in some
specialized direction, in a vocabulary of physics, mathematics,
music, or architecture. Such a boy often enjoys reading
technical books on radio construction, on color photography,

on automobiles, airplanes, or locomotives, on turtles, ants, or snakes, on baseball, skating, or woodcraft. Too many parents believe that every boy must read the standard English classics, ignoring the fact that each has an interest, usually a dozen, any one or all of which can be the incentive for developing a library. Parents who find their young son sequestering a snake in his pocket hope fervently this phase will pass. They fail to realize the rare opportunity afforded to surround him with books on reptiles. He will not read them all, probably go completely through none of them, but get something from each; and as he extends his technical vocabulary of OPHIDIA and then of allied orders, CHELONIA, CROCODILIA, and LACERTILIA, he simultaneously broadens the field in which he enjoys reading.

One boy high in observation, but virtually at the foot of the English-vocabulary scale, scored as high in the knowledge-of-paintings test as many mature teachers of art. At the recommendation of the Laboratory he began buying art books, two a week, read none of them, and yet was not questioned about what he bought. Gradually his interests broadened to furniture, through the discovery of Percy Macquoid, and so to architectural periods and national characteristics, and entirely involuntarily he found himself reading in search of more information about the paintings, furniture, and architectural styles which he now knew well by sight.

Despite the expense of beautifully illustrated volumes, the same advice applies in principle to the boy who can afford no more than a few cents a week. Starting with illustrated catalogues and pamphlets he can build a library of many volumes.

70

As a second step parents should supply the low-vocabulary boy with the JOHNSON O'CONNOR ENGLISH VOCABULARY BUILDER; for to the inevitable question: How can a boy improve his vocabulary? the Laboratory offers this book. It contains 1,118 words arranged in order of familiarity, in the order in which words should be readily learned. In an educational study of thirty scholastically troublesome eighth-grade pupils, in a retarded class, sixty per cent scored below the vocabulary average for their school grade. Twelve months later, after special training based on the VOCABULARY BUILDER, only forty per cent scored below the average for the next grade above. A single year's training of this seriously retarded section, at its own vocabulary level, advanced many of its members to a point from which they went on normally with regular classroom work.

In a high school which administers one of the Laboratory's vocabulary tests at the beginning and again at the end of each school year a junior who wanted to show remarkable improvement in the spring committed to memory some four hundred words from the VOCABULARY BUILDER. It happened that the school chose that spring a test every word of which appears in the book and the boy scored thirty points higher than the previous fall, a remarkable performance. The next fall, the beginning of his senior year, the school administered another of the Laboratory's vocabulary tests but this time one of the more recent forms no word of which appears in the VOCABULARY BUILDER. To the boy's surprise he scored exactly as high as the previous spring. He had pushed a salient into the region of unknown words and without his realizing the consequences had advanced the entire front of his knowledge. This is exactly what the BUILDER should theoretically accomplish and it seems to work practically. The low-vocabulary boy, who wishes to extend his vocabulary rapidly, should begin at the beginning and literally commit to memory the VOCABULARY BUILDER.

71

As a third step, after obtaining the VOCABULARY BUILDER, the low-vocabulary boy should be retested by the Laboratory regularly every two years, for each test appointment stimulates vocabulary improvement. During the first month after a test the average boy improves eight times normal rate as shown in the chart, page 62, of UNSOLVED BUSINESS PROBLEMS. But this temporary impetus peters out in about two years, at which time the low-vocabulary boy should make a second test appointment.

PERIODIC TEST APPOINTMENTS

72

As a fourth step the Laboratory believes that parents should read aloud to the low-vocabulary boy, in order that a single

READING ALOUD defect, often minor, connected perhaps with eyesight, should not delay all of his mental processes; for a boy who scores low in a vocabulary test which he reads for himself frequently scores significantly higher in the same test when the administrator reads each item aloud. In this case the boy's understanding of words, his interests, his own thoughts and reasoning processes, are more advanced than those he gains for himself from the printed page. When, under these conditions, a parent reads aloud, a boy not merely discovers that inspiring ideas come from books but concurrently gains a breadth of knowledge, holds his place in school, and experiences no feeling of inferiority. If, as often happens, the underlying causes of his reading difficulties can later be spotted and overcome, such a boy continues naturally with his own age group, starting his reading at his own age level. Far too often a boy's whole mental outlook is held back to his reading speed; for a boy hampered either by weak eyesight or ineffective reading habits must often restrict his own reading to texts far below his level of understanding and so elementary as neither to hold his interest nor to extend his knowledge background. He soon grows to dislike reading, not only because of its physical requirements but because the subject matter frankly bores him. If demoted in school, because of faulty reading, and so forced to associate with a younger group, he views his handicap with an exaggerated importance and may become so sensitive that he never again faces life normally.

One whose children experience reading difficulties should know John Dewey's essay entitled:

THE PRIMARY-EDUCATION FETICH, first published in the FORUM, May, 1898, and now included as the second selection in his book: EDUCATION TODAY, G. P. Putnam's Sons, 1940.

With the development of motion pictures, of the radio, and of modern museums of all sorts, reading grows less vital even to a well-rounded life. Parents too often exaggerate its importance and so worry about the non-reader as to delay his whole mental development. Certainly great pleasure comes from polished reading, perhaps no more however than from an intelligent hearing of music or from a trained appreciation of art, which many miss without worrying about their loss; and much as enjoyment of these aesthetic pursuits swells with understanding so a grasp of literature comes with effective reading techniques.

73

As a fifth step in helping the low-vocabulary boy parents should send him to some such reading clinic as that operated by Dr.
READING Stella S. Center and Gladys L. Persons at 20
DIFFICULTIES Washington Square North, New York City.
In the introduction to their collection of selected essays called: PROBLEMS IN READING AND THINKING, published by Macmillan Company, 1940, these two inspiring teachers discuss the mechanics of writing, techniques of reading, comprehension, speed, and a program of improvement.

74

As a sixth step parents should keep a low-vocabulary boy in school and in college as long as possible. While no doubt any
FURTHER one can learn words at any time, few adults ex-
EDUCATION pend the needed energy outside the classroom, so that statistically vocabulary correlates with schooling. Ideally the lower a boy's vocabulary the longer should he remain in school to gain that which he lacks. Exactly the reverse happens. The high-vocabulary boy learns rapidly, reads easily, finishes homework without effort, and continues through college, while his low-vocabulary companion leaves school, already disheartened with life.

Great and often discouraging difficulty with college subjects lies ahead of almost every boy low in vocabulary, especially if in addition he chances to score low in accounting aptitude. Such a boy spends longer on written assignments than his classmates and gets little benefit from either the lectures or the prescribed reading. One cannot help feeling that the expedient advice with such a person is to give up all thought of college.

FIGURE 21

ENGINEERING STUDENTS WITH HIGH VOCABULARY SCORES EARN HIGH TUITION REBATES

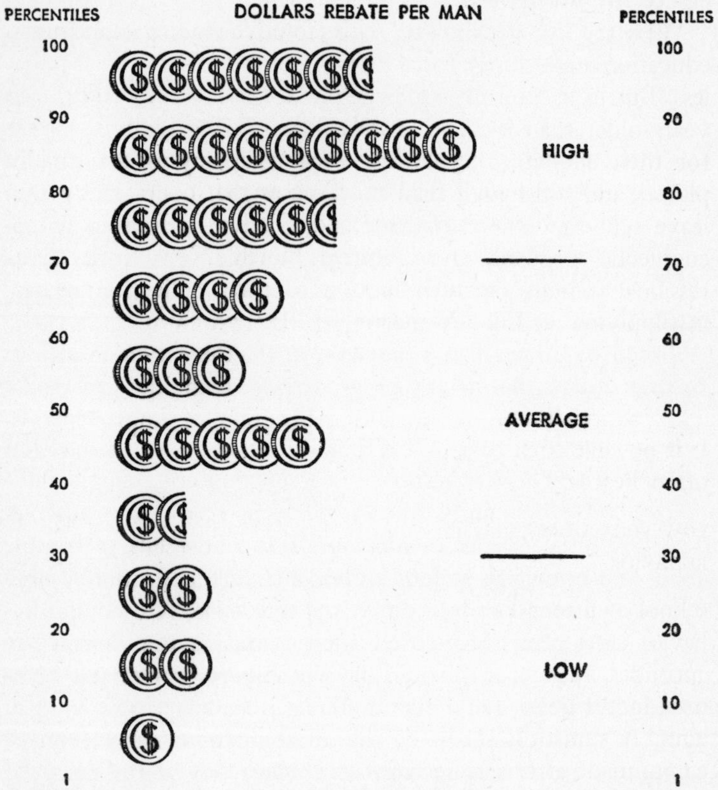

THIS CHART IS BASED ON THE SAME GROUP OF ENGINEERING-SCHOOL STUDENTS AT STEVENS INSTITUTE OF TECHNOLOGY SHOWN IN FIGURE 2, PAGE 6. EACH SYMBOL REPRESENTS TEN DOLLARS AWARDED PER MAN IN TUITION REBATES AS DESCRIBED IN SECTION 1, PAGE 7. AS DISCUSSED MORE FULLY UNDER AGE OF COLLEGE, PAGE 70, STUDENTS EXCEPTIONALLY HIGH IN VOCABULARY, IN THE TOP TENTH, DO LESS WELL THAN THOSE JUST BELOW THEM.

Figure 21 shows diagrammatically the effect of English vocabulary on engineering-school success. In a group of students the bottom third in vocabulary earned only seventeen dollars ($17) per man in tuition rebates, as described more fully earlier on page 7, compared with seventy dollars ($70) per man earned by the top third. Figure 22 shows in similar fashion the effect of English vocabulary and structural visualization combined. Students in the bottom third, judged by composite scores, earned fifteen dollars ($15) per man compared with eighty five dollars ($85) for the top third.

Were the low-vocabulary, retarded boy low also in aptitudes, education might justly force him to leave the classroom as hopeless. But in a carefully studied grade, the retarded boys, two years older than the class as a whole, average slightly higher for their age in structural visualization than those normally placed, and still higher than those advanced. When this group leave school without graduating, the country loses potential engineers, surgeons, and architects, unable to continue professional training partly because of education's ineffectiveness in supplying an English vocabulary.

75

Is it possible to educate a boy beyond his capacity? a question often heard. The Laboratory never encounters a single difficulty known to stem from this cause. A

LOW VOCABULARY
BEHAVIOR

clearer and more frequent source of trouble is lack of effective training. In a public high school of fifteen hundred pupils the twenty most irritating behavior cases resembled closely the student body as a whole in aptitudes, but scored miserably low in vocabulary, the one common factor consistently found among behavior problems at all ages. A statistical study of the trouble makers in a summer camp, made after a tragic mishap as the result of an organized prank, showed them to be the low-vocabulary boys from each cabin, those who felt themselves out of place, who misunderstood the conversation, and who could not get the attention of others at their level.

A picture of the very-low-vocabulary man later in life is that of a college graduate working for a large industrial organization. With every aptitude which should lead to brilliant success, at the 100th percentile in both inductive reasoning and analytical reasoning, above the 95th percentile in structural visualization, and objective in personality, he scored below the

FIGURE 22

ENGINEERING STUDENTS WITH HIGH COMPOSITE VOCABULARY AND STRUCTURAL VISUALIZATION SCORES EARN HIGH TUITION REBATES

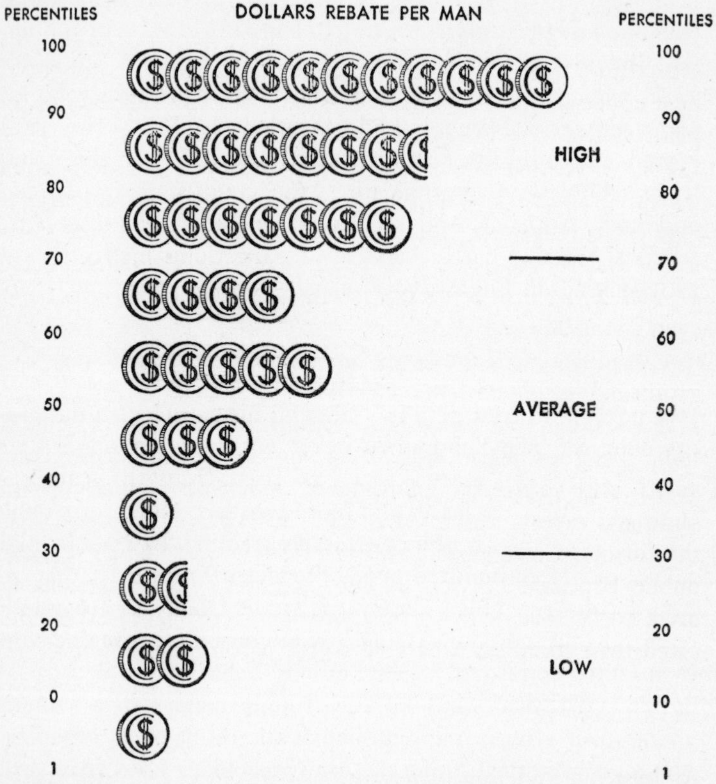

HIGH STRUCTURAL VISUALIZATION COMBINED WITH HIGH VOCABULARY PREDICT ENGINEERING-SCHOOL SUCCESS MORE CONSISTENTLY THAN EITHER TRAIT ALONE. BOYS HIGH IN VOCABU-LARY, FIGURE 21, EARNED $70; THOSE HIGH IN STRUCTURAL VISUALIZATION, FIGURE 2, SLIGHTLY MORE, $77; THOSE HIGH IN THE COMBINATION STILL MORE, $85 APIECE.

5th percentile in vocabulary not only for college men but for all men his age thus far tested. When the company offered its employees voluntary insurance at attractively reduced group rates the low-vocabulary man campaigned against it, despite his less than four months' employment. Patently he had neither read the insurance contract nor understood its significance, but brilliantly high in native aptitudes felt that he should do something spectacular. Several shop foremen declared him too well educated for his inherent capacity. He talked too much, used too many superfluous words, but comprehended little of what was going on. While he had sat impressively through four more years of college than most of the foremen, he actually scored in a nice knowledge of English words, which ought to be a concomitant of education, lower than any foreman in the plant. They were in reality better educated than he.

Far too frequently conscientious parents, who know of some college-graduate failure, decide after anxious consideration to give their own son a more directly applicable vocational training and as they express it to waste no time on a general background. Even in the present unsatisfactory state of education, even though occasionally non-college men succeed where college graduates fail, the latter succeed more often, average as a group higher in salaries and higher in vocabularies.

If vocabulary be taken as a measure of the effect of education, the vocabulary distribution of college graduates compared with a similar plotting of non-college men of the same age reveals a number of the latter better educated than the former. College graduates in title who seem to the general public educated beyond their capabilities prove, when measured, to be men with surprisingly low vocabularies, less educated than countless others who lack parchment diplomas.

76

At least one function of education is instilling a knowledge of the meanings of English words. This cannot be taught effectively to a fifth-grade student and a college freshman in the same room, at the same time. Yet most school grades and even selected sections contain pupils as widely scattered. In several Eastern colleges the lowest members of the freshman class score as low as the average seventh-grade pupil, six years retarded in their understanding of English words. In identically the same class top students score well above the average college senior.

DIVIDING CLASS
INTO SECTIONS

No matter how low a retarded boy scores, he may acquire words at a normal rate if thrown with others who score equally low, for to learn rapidly and permanently one must add words just on the border of one's present knowledge. A boy's difficulties today come from his attempt to work with a group whose vocabularies exceed his own; well-meaning parents annually force low-vocabulary, scholastically-ineffective boys into high-vocabulary schools, where they meet insurmountable barriers. To evade this situation the Laboratory sends low-vocabulary boys to schools where they start at their own level, where the problem of the low-vocabulary boy presents itself with sufficient clarity to be undertaken and solved, where such boys advance exactly as rapidly as those who score higher.

Even in schools which pick their pupils consistently, each class should be taught English in homogeneous groups of selected vocabulary levels. In a specific instance where a medium sized high school divides its sophomore class into six sections, on the basis of the individual vocabulary scores, the top and bottom sections both improve as much as the median students and more than twice as much as the average improvement which the Laboratory finds in other schools.

To gain the same result a preparatory school seats at each table in the dining hall boys of all ages but of identical vocabulary scores, with a resulting buzz of conversation and yearly vocabulary improvement measurably above average. A summer camp tried allotting to each cabin boys of equal vocabulary scores, where formerly it grouped those of an age. The next summer the low-vocabulary group, below the twentieth percentile inspired by a boy at the fifth percentile, organized the camp's musical programs at a level of perfection which the authorities had never achieved.

Most teachers aim too high even in special training and consequently give little or nothing to low-scoring pupils, who often gain more from companions than from a teacher faced with the difficulty of lowering her own vocabulary. Taking advantage of this fact an occasional school assigns to a boy or girl with the characteristics of the teacher, high creative imagination and high inductive reasoning, the special training of low-vocabulary pupils, often with gratifying results.

Few parents realize the extreme simplicity of language implied by the Laboratory's advice to present words just on the boundary of a boy's present knowledge, not too unfamiliar. Even experienced teachers stress mouth-filling words which interest themselves, beyond the acquisitive pupil. Under such conditions, confronted directly with the impossible, the malleable boy becomes painfully discouraged and soon gives the impression of complete inability.

The same boy later in life, in perhaps a routine factory job which he repeats daily, with everyone holding him to standards but no one perpetually pushing, gradually absorbs a knowledge of his surroundings at his own speed and level and ultimately advances, to everyone's surprise. If he still has the aptitudes for the place above he slowly acquires more knowledge from his new position and repeats the process, for advancement in the world does not come annually, at regular intervals, as in school.

77

Low-vocabulary pupils spend longer on each school assignment than those who score high. A group of student nurses, who averaged 135 on the general scale, took four years to complete a three-year course, figure 21, page 132, of THE TOO-MANY-APTITUDE WOMAN. Those who finished nursing training in standard time average 145 on the general scale. An average of ten points lower in vocabulary resulted in thirty per cent more time to perform the same school assignment. This phenomenon leaves low-vocabulary boys and girls no time to devote to strengthening their weak spot; but such figures as the research department can obtain seem to imply that fifteen minutes a day spent regularly at vocabulary building, even at the expense of other lessons, gradually raises vocabulary enough so that in the remaining time one actually accomplishes more. Every additional word, added to a boy's vocabulary, increases at least in theory the amount he accomplishes in any interval. The boy who dislikes school work, who begrudges every minute he devotes to homework, will find that 15 minutes a day spent on vocabulary building soon saves 15 minutes on his lessons.

VOCABULARY AND WORK

PROBLEM VERSUS JOB

The driving urge to leave this human world better than one found it, to reach into the remote unknown and grasp a new idea, may spring from some inherent, unmeasured gift, or come mainly through early training. Whichever the convincing answer, formal education does little to develop the first or supply the last. High-school and preparatory-school faculties, perhaps of necessity, concentrate on college preparation; while many inspired teachers lack structural visualization, a primal part of the problem-solving instinct. Even the mathematical examples propounded by a majority of textbooks are rarely true problems in the legitimate sense of that word; to the experienced scientist, a problem once clearly put in precise language is virtually solved; in actual research the foremost chores are stating the question, and then culling from a miscellaneous heap of irrelevant data the illusive pertinent facts.

As distinct from true research, the CENTURY DICTIONARY describes a job as an undertaking of a defined or restricted character. Monotonous, uninspiring jobs must be done, both in school and in life, particularly during national emergencies, when the country calls for equipment in excess of normal, airplanes, machine tools, army trucks. At the moment of writing, aviation clamors for ground mechanics to perform a type of work undreamt of half a century ago, and one which by the same token will no doubt sometime pass into oblivion; for the more defined a job becomes by repetition the more certainly will an automatic machine sometime do it both faster and with greater precision than the human being. The high-school or college graduate who takes a prescribed job, with its momentary and apparent certainty, must face its almost inevitable disappearance within the next twenty years, often at about the time he reaches an age at which he cannot start again in a new direction. Mechanical changes and industrial fluctuations cause the laying off of vast numbers of job holders, many of whom never again find permanent employment. Boys high in structural visualization, who might solve real problems, should not be satisfied to perform permanently a repetitive job which might be done equally well by a less gifted person or even by an ingenious machine.

A laborious job and a tantalizing problem, as the Laboratory uses the words, differ not in the relative difficulty of the two, but essentially in the number of times each has been done before. In automobile manufacture the putting of a particular nut on a given bolt several hundred times a day is in this terminology a job, done often enough so that its performance involves no problem. Unearthing and deciphering another Ptolemaic papyrus from the wealth of material protected by the arid Egyptian soil is today a job in much the same sense. The task has now been done often enough so that while still difficult it is not, in the opinion of Arnold F. Toynbee, STUDY OF HISTORY, pages 5 and 6, so formidable a problem as understanding the Seleucid Monarchy, virtually untouched for lack of materials. Much as a boy turns to a defined and restricted job with a sense of security, so historians turn to Egypt.

Once the United States owned enough undeveloped land to grant every ambitious boy a homestead at the physical frontier of the country. Here he met daily problems. Gradually he cleared the land, improved the farms, developed tractors, so that while not long ago fourteen persons on the land fed themselves and only one in a city, now one on a farm feeds himself and three city dwellers.

With the gradual passing of this frontier life and the need of great physical exertion boys turned to so-called 'WHITE COLLAR' jobs, not as sometimes stated for fear of work, for the land never lacked volunteers ready to brave the untold hardships of tilling primeval ground. Boys flocked to the city for opportunities. Now, the mechanization of bookkeeping and the improved handling of clerical routine reduce even office work. The oft-suggested return to physical labor is not the solution despite temporary, local calls.

To exert his every aptitude the gifted boy must seek a new frontier, for only the hardships of exploring present unlimited challenge. Since physical frontiers no longer exist, the Laboratory suggests attacking the frontier of human understanding, a vast unknown region for the born pioneer.

Too many parents assume as axiomatic that only the endowed genius should consider a problem and advise the boy who does poorly in formal schooling, who ultimately fails, to seek a clerical job because they believe such a position easy to find and hold. Yet here he competes instantly and constantly with a multitude of clerks in a field which to him is extremely distasteful. The same boy may find in some unexplored direction an opportunity where, incredible as it seems, he rarely competes with others. One such boy holds a place in the scientific world because of his skilful handling and intimate study of reptiles. Another photographs and collects geological specimens from inaccessible parts of the world. Each such undertaking interests only one person in many thousands and clearly no brochure can discuss them all.

Earning a livelihood at some new outpost of knowledge is as much a part of the problem as when the born pioneer, who turned West a century ago, put his hand to every task. Today the explorer for knowledge need not literally raise his own food, physically build his own house, weave his clothes with his own hands, but he must recognize that gaining his food and clothing is as much a part of pioneering as in the days of the land frontier.

The American Telephone and Telegraph Company through the Bell Laboratory spent, during the year 1940, twelve million dollars on research. Other large corporations, the General Electric Company and the General Motors Corporation, to name but two illustrations, spend on research sums which gradually increase from one decade to another. The Rockefeller Foundation, the Carnegie Foundation, and literally nearly a thousand other similar groups, help individual scientists to an extent which varies from year to year but gradually mounts. Universities spend constantly growing appropriations on research. A boy, not primarily intent on amassing money, but challenged by research, often finds here a more certain and lasting income than can the average clerk in a 'WHITE COLLAR' job.

A boy who starts with a list of confined jobs, in considering his life's work, inevitably turns to a stereotyped groove. By starting instead with a list of his own aptitudes, arranged in order of their preeminence, he more frequently imagines and ultimately creates an undertaking which uses them all in the order of their importance to him as an individual. In so doing he should virtually neglect the actual scores and letter grades, using them only for the sake of gaining their relative order.

The philosophy of the Human Engineering Laboratory stresses the need of surveying one's own capabilities, not with some fixed job in mind, but with the aim of making that peculiar contribution to the world of which one alone is capable, of planning life from the beginning about one's aptitudes, of reaching constantly for progress to give them ampler expression. Continued happiness, great achievement, the author believes depend upon defining clearly, early in life, a goal for which one has the needed aptitudes, but so remote, so visionary, that one can ever approach more closely without arriving.

SIZE OF COLLEGE

Section 50, page 86, discusses at length the Laboratory's belief that in weighing the various factors which determine a boy's choice of college as near an absolute rule as can be laid down is that one low in accounting aptitude should not go to a large institution but find instead a small, friendly, intimate student body. Here a boy who shows his worst side on paper learns to express himself directly both in the informal classroom atmosphere and in evening discussions with faculty members, low accounting aptitude taking its proper place as no more than one aspect of total capacity.

Conversely, another boy high in the aptitude should in the Laboratory's opinion attend a large college. Though he may relish for a time the sense of his own excellence as compared with classmates who go clerically more slowly, the ease of a small group offers him less challenge; and to succeed a boy must exert to the full every trait he possesses. Parents are the inexcusable stumbling block. Eager for their son's prowess they underrate his capabilities, and send him to a small college for fear he will not survive in the larger competition. In consequence he never meets a situation comparable with his ability, and becomes another many-aptitude failure.

The approximate student bodies shown in the three following tables change from one year to the next, and are never strictly commensurate. One college devotes itself exclusively to its own students; another shares faculty members with a girls' school in the same city and so acquires a student body equivalent to the sum of those listed under separate names. One builds its graduate school on a detached campus with an autonomous organization; another mells it indistinguishably with the undergraduate group.

In general boys low in accounting aptitude, grades C− and D, at the thirtieth percentile and below, should select a college from the smallest third, marked in the following tables as: SUGGESTED TO ACCOUNTING APTITUDE, LOW; boys high in accounting aptitude, grades $B+$ and A, above the seventieth percentile, should select a college from the largest third, suggested to ACCOUNTING APTITUDE, HIGH. Boys who in Laboratory terminology rank AVERAGE in accounting aptitude, between the thirty-first and seventieth percentiles, grades B and C. should select a college from the middle third in size.

TECHNICAL OR GENERAL

Part II entitled STRUCTURAL VISUALIZATION, pages 5 to 46, deals largely with the choice between a technical institute and liberal arts or general college. The extremely subjective boy interested in engineering, who grades A in structural visualization, should with little or no hesitation prepare for a technical school such as those listed in table VIII. If attracted by pure research rather than engineering he may choose between a technical school and a science concentration in a more general college. The objective and extremely objective boy, pages 57 to 71, has no such easy option. If grade A in structural visualization he must at some point during his education gain either a science or engineering background. He may do this as an undergraduate in one of the technical schools of table VIII or after three or four years of academic collegiate work.

One who grades B in structural visualization may possess the trait to exactly the same degree as another who grades A; or less often, because of the inaccuracies of the current tests, may lack the trait completely. For safety the Laboratory believes that one interested in engineering, who grades B in structural visualization, should seek his engineering degree in a general university, not in a purely technical school. The following tables group colleges first by structural visualization, and then within these types by approximate size of student body.

AGE OF COLLEGE

Less tangible in its significance than either size or type is the age of an institution. Knowing that colleges vary in language requirements both for entrance and for survival, the Laboratory must ultimately measure the vocabulary level of each and recommend in accord with such findings, sending high-vocabulary students to high-vocabulary schools, low students to low-vocabulary schools. But this represents years of work for a large research staff; and with every shift of college administration, to a slight extent with every faculty resignation or appointment, comes a change in language emphasis. Still further the present variation from one school to another is less than the Laboratory believes desirable and in consequence can be used only as a trend to exaggerate.

Judgments among staff members as to language levels differ too radically to form a consistent basis. Rather than assign a purely arbitrary section of the vocabulary scale to each college, the author assumes that as an institution ages it tends to rise in vocabulary, the freshmen in the old established colleges averaging higher than in those more recently founded.

The true academic standing of a college depends on the amount it gives, on the difference between its enrolling freshmen and its graduating seniors. Autocratic selection of freshmen, high vocabulary at entrance, does not necessarily go hand in hand with rapid progress thereafter; schools where freshmen start low may graduate seniors who score high. The reader who spots some divergence from his own opinion in the following tables may be thinking of the total student body. Whatever rule the Laboratory adopts for its own guidance applies solely to matriculating freshmen; for the vocabulary of upper classmen rests with the school and its educational contribution.

Since students of a similar vocabulary level learn rapidly together the Laboratory must be consistent at least in its own advice; in one instance it tested as individuals more than fifty members of an entering class, a group large enough to make its own level felt and so to advance at maximum speed. Scatter among students of the same age and grade far exceeds the variation from one college to another. Should the Laboratory send to the same college a student from the top of the scale and another from the bottom, the mistake would overshadow that of sending either at random anywhere. Consistency in the Laboratory's counsel is therefore a prime requisite.

For boys who score high in English vocabulary, *A* or *B*+ in terms of school grade, above the seventieth percentile, the

Laboratory recommends a college in the oldest third. For boys low in vocabulary as judged by their place in school, grade C— or D, the Laboratory recommends a college in the third most recently founded, in the confirmed belief that such boys will graduate with vocabularies significantly higher than if they attend an older school. For boys average in vocabulary the Laboratory recommends a college in the middle third in age.

TABLE VIII

Technical Colleges

COLLEGE AND LOCATION DATE FOUNDED	APPROXIMATE STUDENT BODY

Suggested to: Structural Visualization, Grade A (Men's Norms); Accounting Aptitude, High (Men's Norms); English Vocabulary, High.

POLYTECHNIC INSTITUTE OF BROOKLYN 1854 Brooklyn, New York	2,900
MICHIGAN STATE COLLEGE OF AGRICULTURE AND APPLIED SCIENCE 1855 East Lansing, Michigan	6,600
IOWA STATE COLLEGE OF AGRICULTURE AND MECHANIC ARTS 1858 Ames, Iowa	7,100
MASSACHUSETTS INSTITUTE OF TECHNOLOGY 1861 Cambridge, Massachusetts	3,100
AGRICULTURAL AND MECHANICAL COLLEGE OF TEXAS 1862 College Station, Texas	6,350
KANSAS STATE COLLEGE OF AGRICULTURE AND APPLIED SCIENCE 1863 Manhattan, Kansas	4,300
OREGON STATE COLLEGE 1868 Corvallis, Oregon	5,000
ALABAMA POLYTECHNIC INSTITUTE 1872 Auburn, Alabama	3,500
VIRGINIA POLYTECHNIC INSTITUTE 1872 Blacksburg, Virginia	3,000

Suggested to: Structural Visualization, Grade A (Men's Norms); Accounting Aptitude, High (Men's Norms); English Vocabulary, Average.

GEORGIA SCHOOL OF TECHNOLOGY 1885 Atlanta, Georgia	2,700

TABLE VIII CONTINUED

COLLEGE AND LOCATION DATE FOUNDED	APPROXIMATE STUDENT BODY

Continued: Structural Visualization, Grade A (Men's Norms); Accounting Aptitude, High (Men's Norms); English Vocabulary, Average.

UTAH STATE AGRICULTURAL COLLEGE 1888   3,200
  Logan, Utah

STATE COLLEGE OF WASHINGTON 1890   4,250
  Pullman, Washington

OKLAHOMA AGRICULTURAL AND MECHANICAL   6,350
  COLLEGE 1891 Stillwater, Oklahoma

Suggested to: Structural Visualization, Grade A (Men's Norms); Accounting Aptitude, High (Men's Norms); English Vocabulary, Low.

CARNEGIE INSTITUTE OF TECHNOLOGY 1900   3,350
  Pittsburgh, Pennsylvania

TEXAS TECHNOLOGICAL COLLEGE 1923   3,900
  Lubbock, Texas

Suggested to: Structural Visualization, Grade A (Men's Norms); Accounting Aptitude, Average (Men's Norms); English Vocabulary, High.

RENSSELAER POLYTECHNIC INSTITUTE 1824   1,500
  Troy, New York

COOPER UNION 1859   1,200
  New York, New York

MISSISSIPPI STATE COLLEGE 1878   2,250
  State College, Mississippi

COLORADO STATE COLLEGE OF AGRICULTURE AND   1,900
  MECHANIC ARTS 1879 (1870) Fort Collins, Colorado

Suggested to: Structural Visualization, Grade A (Men's Norms); Accounting Aptitude, Average (Men's Norms); English Vocabulary, Average.

CASE SCHOOL OF APPLIED SCIENCE 1880   1,450
  Cleveland, Ohio

NEWARK COLLEGE OF ENGINEERING 1881   1,800
  Newark, New Jersey

NORTH CAROLINA STATE COLLEGE OF AGRICULTURE   2,200
  AND ENGINEERING 1889 Raleigh, North Carolina

TABLE VIII CONTINUED

COLLEGE AND LOCATION DATE FOUNDED	APPROXIMATE STUDENT BODY

Continued: Structural Visualization, Grade A (Men's Norms); Accounting Aptitude, Average (Men's Norms); English Vocabulary, Average.

NORTH DAKOTA AGRICULTURAL COLLEGE 1890 Fargo, North Dakota	1,800
DREXEL INSTITUTE OF TECHNOLOGY 1891 Philadelphia, Pennsylvania	1,900
DETROIT INSTITUTE OF TECHNOLOGY 1891 Detroit, Michigan	1,800

Suggested to: Structural Visualization, Grade A (Men's Norms); Accounting Aptitude, Low (Men's Norms); English Vocabulary, Low.

ARMOUR COLLEGE OF ENGINEERING 1892 Chicago, Illinois	1,850
MONTANA STATE COLLEGE 1893 Bozeman, Montana	1,700
CLEMSON AGRICULTURAL COLLEGE 1893 (1889) Clemson, South Carolina	2,200
LOUISIANA POLYTECHNIC INSTITUTE 1894 Ruston, Louisiana	2,000
BRADLEY POLYTECHNIC INSTITUTE 1896 Peoria, Illinois	1,400

Suggested to: Structural Visualization, Grade A (Men's Norms); Accounting Aptitude, Low (Men's Norms); English Vocabulary, High.

WORCESTER POLYTECHNIC INSTITUTE 1865 Worcester, Massachusetts	675
STEVENS INSTITUTE OF TECHNOLOGY 1867 Hoboken, New Jersey	750
COLORADO SCHOOL OF MINES 1870 Golden, Colorado	850
MISSOURI SCHOOL OF MINES AND METALLURGY 1871 Rolla, Missouri	800
ROSE POLYTECHNIC INSTITUTE 1874 Terre Haute, Indiana	275

TABLE VIII CONTINUED

COLLEGE AND LOCATION DATE FOUNDED	APPROXIMATE STUDENT BODY

Suggested to: Structural Visualization, Grade A (Men's Norms); Accounting Aptitude, Low (Men's Norms); English Vocabulary, Average.

SOUTH DAKOTA STATE COLLEGE OF AGRICULTURE AND   1,150
  MECHANIC ARTS 1881 (1883) Brookings, South Dakota

TRI-STATE COLLEGE 1884   875
  Angola, Indiana

SOUTH DAKOTA STATE SCHOOL OF MINES 1885   400
  Rapid City, South Dakota

MICHIGAN COLLEGE OF MINING AND TECHNOLOGY 1885   825
  Houghton, Michigan

PRATT INSTITUTE 1887   500
  Brooklyn, New York

NEW MEXICO SCHOOL OF MINES 1889   100
  Socorro, New Mexico

NEW MEXICO COLLEGE OF AGRICULTURE AND   1,050
  MECHANIC ARTS 1889 State College, New Mexico

WEBB INSTITUTE OF NAVAL ARCHITECTURE 1889   75
  New York, New York

CALIFORNIA INSTITUTE OF TECHNOLOGY 1891   875
  Pasadena, California

Suggested to: Structural Visualization, Grade A (Men's Norms); Accounting Aptitude, Average (Men's Norms); English Vocabulary, Low.

RHODE ISLAND STATE COLLEGE 1892   1,150
  Kingston, Rhode Island

MONTANA SCHOOL OF MINES 1895 (1893)   325
  Butte, Montana

THOMAS S. CLARKSON MEMORIAL COLLEGE OF   575
  TECHNOLOGY 1896 Potsdam, New York

TEXAS COLLEGE OF MINES AND METALLURGY 1913   1,100
  El Paso, Texas

TENNESSEE POLYTECHNIC INSTITUTE 1915   975
  Cookeville, Tennessee

END OF TABLE VIII

TABLE IX

Coeducational Colleges and Universities Offering Courses in Engineering

(Most Men's Colleges, Table x, also give Courses in Engineering or the Exact Sciences.)

COLLEGE AND LOCATION DATE FOUNDED	APPROXIMATE STUDENT BODY

Suggested to: Structural Visualization, Grade B (Men's Norms); Accounting Aptitude, High (Men's Norms); English Vocabulary, High.

UNIVERSITY OF PENNSYLVANIA 1740 Philadelphia, Pennsylvania	11,300
COLUMBIA UNIVERSITY 1754 New York, New York	17,000
UNIVERSITY OF PITTSBURGH 1787 Pittsburgh, Pennsylvania	12,400
UNIVERSITY OF MICHIGAN 1817 Ann Arbor, Michigan	12,600
UNIVERSITY OF CINCINNATI 1819 Cincinnati, Ohio	11,500
NEW YORK UNIVERSITY 1831 New York, New York	36,200
COLLEGE OF THE CITY OF NEW YORK 1847 New York, New York	26,000
STATE UNIVERSITY OF IOWA 1847 Iowa City, Iowa	7,400
UNIVERSITY OF WISCONSIN 1848 (1836) Madison, Wisconsin	12,000
NORTHWESTERN UNIVERSITY 1851 Evanston, Illinois	16,000

Suggested to: Structural Visualization, Grade B (Men's Norms); Accounting Aptitude, High (Men's Norms); English Vocabulary, Average.

WASHINGTON UNIVERSITY 1853 St. Louis, Missouri	7,100
PENNSYLVANIA STATE COLLEGE 1855 State College, Pennsylvania	7,150

TABLE IX CONTINUED

COLLEGE AND LOCATION DATE FOUNDED	APPROXIMATE STUDENT BODY

Continued: Structural Visualization, Grade B (Men's Norms); Accounting Aptitude, High (Men's Norms); English Vocabulary, Average.

LOUISIANA STATE UNIVERSITY 1860 (1845) Baton Rouge, Louisiana	8,200
UNIVERSITY OF WASHINGTON 1861 Seattle, Washington	12,100
UNIVERSITY OF ILLINOIS 1867 Urbana, Illinois	15,100
UNIVERSITY OF CALIFORNIA 1868 (1855) Berkeley and Los Angeles, California	25,300
UNIVERSITY OF MINNESOTA 1868 (1851) Minneapolis, Minnesota	17,400
UNIVERSITY OF NEBRASKA 1869 Lincoln, Nebraska	7,400
SYRACUSE UNIVERSITY 1870 (1849) Syracuse, New York	8,400

Suggested to: Structural Visualization, Grade B (Men's Norms); Accounting Aptitude, High (Men's Norms); English Vocabulary, Low.

OHIO STATE UNIVERSITY 1872 (1870) Columbus, Ohio	15,950
UNIVERSITY OF SOUTHERN CALIFORNIA 1880 Los Angeles, California	7,300
UNIVERSITY OF TEXAS 1883 (1881) Austin, Texas	11,500
WAYNE UNIVERSITY 1929 Detroit, Michigan	13,000

Suggested to: Structural Visualization, Grade B (Men's Norms); Accounting Aptitude, Average (Men's Norms); English Vocabulary, High.

RUTGERS UNIVERSITY 1766 New Brunswick, New Jersey	5,350
UNIVERSITY OF GEORGIA 1785 Athens, Georgia	3,500
UNIVERSITY OF TENNESSEE 1794 Knoxville, Tennessee	4,900

TABLE IX CONTINUED

COLLEGE AND LOCATION DATE FOUNDED	APPROXIMATE STUDENT BODY

Continued: Structural Visualization, Grade B (Men's Norms); Accounting Aptitude, Average (Men's Norms); English Vocabulary, High.

UNIVERSITY OF MARYLAND 1807 College Park, Maryland	4,500
GEORGE WASHINGTON UNIVERSITY 1821 Washington, D. C.	6,800
UNIVERSITY OF ALABAMA 1831 (1820) Tuscaloosa, Alabama	5,200
TULANE UNIVERSITY OF LOUISIANA 1834 New Orleans, Louisiana	4,600
UNIVERSITY OF LOUISVILLE 1837 Louisville, Kentucky	4,000
DUKE UNIVERSITY 1838 Durham, North Carolina	3,600
UNIVERSITY OF MISSOURI 1839 Columbia, Missouri	6,200
UNIVERSITY OF ROCHESTER 1850 Rochester, New York	3,200
UNIVERSITY OF UTAH 1850 Salt Lake City, Utah	4,500

Suggested to: Structural Visualization, Grade B (Men's Norms); Accounting Aptitude, Average (Men's Norms); English Vocabulary, Average.

UNIVERSITY OF DENVER 1864 Denver, Colorado	3,800
CORNELL UNIVERSITY 1865 Ithaca, New York	7,000
UNIVERSITY OF KENTUCKY 1865 Lexington, Kentucky	4,100
UNIVERSITY OF KANSAS 1866 Lawrence, Kansas	4,700
WEST VIRGINIA UNIVERSITY 1867 Morgantown, West Virginia	3,200
PURDUE UNIVERSITY 1869 Lafayette, Indiana	7,000

TABLE IX CONTINUED

COLLEGE AND LOCATION DATE FOUNDED	APPROXIMATE STUDENT BODY

Suggested to: Structural Visualization, Grade B (Men's Norms); Accounting Aptitude, Average (Men's Norms); English Vocabulary, Low.

UNIVERSITY OF COLORADO 1876 (1861) Boulder, Colorado	4,500
UNIVERSITY OF DETROIT 1877 Detroit, Michigan	3,300
MARQUETTE UNIVERSITY 1881 (1855) Milwaukee, Wisconsin	4,200
STANFORD UNIVERSITY 1885 Palo Alto, California	4,600
UNIVERSITY OF OKLAHOMA 1890 Norman, Oklahoma	7,000
SOUTHERN METHODIST UNIVERSITY 1911 Dallas, Texas	3,400

Suggested to: Structural Visualization, Grade B (Men's Norms); Accounting Aptitude, Low (Men's Norms); English Vocabulary, High.

UNIVERSITY OF DELAWARE 1743 Newark, Delaware	950
BROWN UNIVERSITY 1764 Providence, Rhode Island	2,000
UNIVERSITY OF VERMONT 1791 Burlington, Vermont	1,400
UNIVERSITY OF SOUTH CAROLINA 1801 Columbia, South Carolina	1,900
UNIVERSITY OF VIRGINIA 1819 Charlottesville, Virginia	2,900
ALFRED UNIVERSITY 1836 Alfred, New York	625
UNIVERSITY OF MISSISSIPPI 1844 University, Mississippi	1,300
BUCKNELL UNIVERSITY 1846 Lewisburg, Pennsylvania	1,300
TUFTS COLLEGE 1852 Medford, Massachusetts	2,100

TABLE IX CONTINUED

COLLEGE AND LOCATION DATE FOUNDED	APPROXIMATE STUDENT BODY

Suggested to: Structural Visualization, Grade B (Men's Norms); Accounting Aptitude, Low (Men's Norms); English Vocabulary, Average.

VALPARAISO UNIVERSITY 1859	500
Valparaiso, Indiana	
SWARTHMORE COLLEGE 1864	725
Swarthmore, Pennsylvania	
UNIVERSITY OF MAINE 1865	1,900
Orono, Maine	
UNIVERSITY OF NEW HAMPSHIRE 1866	2,000
Durham, New Hampshire	
UNIVERSITY OF AKRON 1870	1,700
Akron, Ohio	
OHIO NORTHERN UNIVERSITY 1871	800
Ada, Ohio	

Suggested to: Structural Visualization, Grade B (Men's Norms); Accounting Aptitude, Low (Men's Norms); English Vocabulary, Low.

UNIVERSITY OF ARKANSAS 1872	2,800
Fayetteville, Arkansas	
UNIVERSITY OF THE CITY OF TOLEDO 1872	2,200
Toledo, Ohio	
VANDERBILT UNIVERSITY 1872	1,800
Nashville, Tennessee	
UNIVERSITY OF NEVADA 1874	1,250
Reno, Nevada	
FENN COLLEGE 1881	2,800
Cleveland, Ohio	
UNIVERSITY OF CONNECTICUT 1881	1,250
Storrs, Connecticut	
UNIVERSITY OF NORTH DAKOTA 1883	2,000
Grand Forks, North Dakota	
UNIVERSITY OF ARIZONA 1885	2,900
Tucson, Arizona	
UNIVERSITY OF WYOMING 1887	2,200
Laramie, Wyoming	

TABLE IX CONTINUED

COLLEGE AND LOCATION DATE FOUNDED	APPROXIMATE STUDENT BODY

Continued: Structural Visualization, Grade B (Men's Norms); Accounting Aptitude, Low (Men's Norms); English Vocabulary, Low.

CATHOLIC UNIVERSITY OF AMERICA 1887 Washington, D. C.	2,100
UNIVERSITY OF IDAHO 1889 Moscow, Idaho	3,000
UNIVERSITY OF NEW MEXICO 1892 (1889) Albuquerque, New Mexico	1,800
UNIVERSITY OF TULSA 1894 Tulsa, Oklahoma	1,100
RICE INSTITUTE 1912 (1891) Houston, Texas	1,400
UNIVERSITY OF ALASKA 1915 College, Alaska	300

TABLE X

MEN'S COLLEGES AND UNIVERSITIES

COLLEGE AND LOCATION DATE FOUNDED	APPROXIMATE STUDENT BODY

Suggested to: Structural Visualization, Grade C or D (Men's Norms); Accounting Aptitude, High (Men's Norms); English Vocabulary, High.

HARVARD UNIVERSITY 1636 Cambridge, Massachusetts	8,500
YALE UNIVERSITY 1701 New Haven, Connecticut	5,300
PRINCETON UNIVERSITY 1746 Princeton, New Jersey	2,700
DARTMOUTH COLLEGE 1769 Hanover, New Hampshire	2,400

Suggested to: Structural Visualization, Grade C or D (Men's Norms); Accounting Aptitude, High (Men's Norms); English Vocabulary, Average.

COLGATE UNIVERSITY 1819 Hamilton, New York	1,100

TABLE X CONTINUED

COLLEGE AND LOCATION DATE FOUNDED	APPROXIMATE STUDENT BODY

Continued: Structural Visualization, Grade C or D (Men's Norms); Accounting Aptitude, High (Men's Norms); English Vocabulary, Average.

WAKE FOREST COLLEGE   1833   1,050
   Wake Forest, North Carolina

Suggested to: Structural Visualization, Grade C or D (Men's Norms); Accounting Aptitude, High (Men's Norms); English Vocabulary, Low.

EMORY UNIVERSITY   1836   1,450
   Atlanta, Georgia

UNIVERSITY OF NOTRE DAME DU LAC   1843 (1842)   3,200
   Notre Dame, Indiana

MANHATTAN COLLEGE   1849   1,250
   New York, New York

UNIVERSITY OF FLORIDA   1853   3,400
   Gainesville, Florida

LEHIGH UNIVERSITY   1865   2,000
   Bethlehem, Pennsylvania

JOHNS HOPKINS UNIVERSITY   1867   1,600
   Baltimore, Maryland

NORTHEASTERN UNIVERSITY   1898   5,900
   Boston, Massachusetts

Suggested to: Structural Visualization, Grade C or D (Men's Norms); Accounting Aptitude, Average (Men's Norms); English Vocabulary, High.

WASHINGTON AND LEE UNIVERSITY   1749   950
   Lexington, Virginia

UNIVERSITY OF SANTA CLARA   1777   525
   Santa Clara, California

WASHINGTON AND JEFFERSON COLLEGE   1780   550
   Washington, Pennsylvania

UNION COLLEGE   1785   800
   Schenectady, New York

WILLIAMS COLLEGE   1785   825
   Williamstown, Massachusetts

FRANKLIN AND MARSHALL COLLEGE   1787   925
   Lancaster, Pennsylvania

TABLE X CONTINUED

COLLEGE AND LOCATION DATE FOUNDED	APPROXIMATE STUDENT BODY

Continued: Structural Visualization, Grade C or D (Men's Norms); Accounting Aptitude, Average (Men's Norms); English Vocabulary, High.

BOWDOIN COLLEGE 1794 Brunswick, Maine	650

Suggested to: Structural Visualization, Grade C or D (Men's Norms); Accounting Aptitude, Average (Men's Norms); English Vocabulary, Average.

AMHERST COLLEGE 1821 Amherst, Massachusetts	875
TRINITY COLLEGE 1823 Hartford, Connecticut	550
LAFAYETTE COLLEGE 1826 Easton, Pennsylvania	950
WESLEYAN UNIVERSITY 1831 Middletown, Connecticut	750

Suggested to: Structural Visualization, Grade C or D (Men's Norms); Accounting Aptitude, Average (Men's Norms); English Vocabulary, Low.

DAVIDSON COLLEGE 1837 Davidson, North Carolina	675
VILLANOVA COLLEGE 1842 Villanova, Pennsylvania	950
MUHLENBERG COLLEGE 1848 Allentown, Pennsylvania	525
WOFFORD COLLEGE 1851 Spartanburg, South Carolina	500
SPRINGFIELD COLLEGE 1885 Springfield, Massachusetts	550
GONZAGA UNIVERSITY 1889 Spokane, Washington	825

Suggested to: Structural Visualization, Grade C or D (Men's Norms); Accounting Aptitude, Low (Men's Norms); English Vocabulary, High.

HAMPDEN-SYDNEY COLLEGE 1776 Hampden Sydney, Virginia	375
SAINT JOHN'S COLLEGE 1784 Annapolis, Maryland	175

TABLE X CONTINUED

COLLEGE AND LOCATION DATE FOUNDED	APPROXIMATE STUDENT BODY

Suggested to: Structural Visualization, Grade C or D (Men's Norms); Accounting Aptitude, Low (Men's Norms); English Vocabulary, Average.

HAMILTON COLLEGE 1812 Clinton, New York	425
HOBART COLLEGE 1822 Geneva, New York	375
KENYON COLLEGE 1824 Gambier, Ohio	300
MISSISSIPPI COLLEGE 1826 Clinton, Mississippi	425
RANDOLPH-MACON COLLEGE 1830 Ashland, Virginia	325
WABASH COLLEGE 1832 Crawfordsville, Indiana	425
HAVERFORD COLLEGE 1833 Haverford, Pennsylvania	325

Suggested to: Structural Visualization, Grade C or D (Men's Norms); Accounting Aptitude, Low (Men's Norms); English Vocabulary, Low.

WESTMINSTER COLLEGE 1851 Fulton, Missouri	325
UNIVERSITY OF THE SOUTH 1858 Sewanee, Tennessee	300
BARD COLLEGE 1860 Annandale-on-Hudson, New York	100
DREW UNIVERSITY 1867 Madison, New Jersey	425
SAINT EDWARD'S UNIVERSITY 1885 Austin, Texas	225
CLARK UNIVERSITY 1887 Worcester, Massachusetts	375

INDEX

accidents
  industrial, 28
accounting
  characteristics used, 15
  creative imagination, 16
  structural visualization, low, 7, 8,
    9, 12, 13
accounting aptitude
  accuracy, 117
  acquired or inherited, 112
  banking, 74
  exceeds structural visualization, 10
  experience, 75
  grades A, C, D, 16
  growth, 75, 117
  high, 77
  independence, 77, 117
  percentile ratio, 41
  reliability, 23
  retarded students, 44
  sex difference, 75, 77
  teaching, 16
  training, 75
  worksample 1, 75
  worksample 267, 76
  worksample 268, 75, 76
accounting aptitude, average, uses
  educational advising, 91
  high-school teaching, 91
  preparatory-school teaching, 91
  selling laboratory materials, 93
  teaching, 91
accounting-aptitude correlations
  inductive reasoning, 77, 97
  listed, 77
accounting aptitude, high, uses
  accounting, 12, 13, 15
  actuarial work, 15
  adding-machine operation, 15
  algebra, 78, 80
  architecture, 14, 88
  arithmetic, 78
  astronomy (mathematical), 14
  astrophysics, 14
  bachelor-of-art degree, 81
  banking, 10, 11, 12, 13, 47, 74
  banking executive work, 15

accounting aptitude, high, uses
  banking (teller), 15
  bookkeeping, 15
  building management, 60
  business management, 60
  business research, 15
  city management, 60
  clerical work, 15
  community housing, 14
  consulting engineering, 14
  contracting, 14
  corporation law, 15
  cost accounting, 11, 14
  dining-hall supervision, 60
  economics, 15
  engineering executive work, 60
  estimating, 11, 14
  executive secretarial work, 15
  executive work, 60
  factory management, 60
  heredity studies, 77
  hospital management, 60
  housing management, 60
  manufacturing executive work,
    58, 60
  material surveys, 11
  mathematics, 78
  museum management, 60
  nursing, 54
  nutrition (laboratory research),
    54
  personal secretarial work, 15
  piano, 110, 111
  population studies, 15, 77
  quantity surveys, 14
  statistics, 77
  stenography, 15, 78
  store management, 60
  typing, 15, 78
accounting aptitude, low
  remedial steps, 83
  small schools, 86
accounting aptitude, low, and
  structural visualization, 78
accounting aptitude, low, uses
  agriculture, 14
  airplane design, 14

PUBLICATIONS

BOOKS

For the general reader

Johnson O'Connor English Vocabulary Builder, Two Volumes
Human Engineering Laboratory, 1948　　　　$10.00 *per volume*
Square Pegs in Square Holes *by Margaret E. Broadley*
Doubleday, 1946　　　　$2.50
Know Your Real Abilities *by Charles V. and Margaret E. Broadley*
McGraw Hill, 1948　　　　$3.50
Hur man upptäcker sina *verkliga* anlag *av Charles och Margaret Broadley*
Biblioteksförlaget, Stockholm, 1949

Concerning the grammar-school pupil as well as the adult

Aptitudes and the Languages *by Johnson O'Connor*
Human Engineering Laboratory, 1944　　　　$2.00

Concerning.the high-school and college student as well as the adult

Structural Visualization *by Johnson O'Connor*
Human Engineering Laboratory, 1942　　　　$2.75
The Too-Many-Aptitude Woman *by Johnson O'Connor*
Human Engineering Laboratory, 1941　　　　$4.00
The Unique Individual *by Johnson O'Connor*
Human Engineering Laboratory, 1947　　　　$4.00

Concerning primarily the problems of the adult

Unsolved Business Problems *by Johnson O'Connor*
Human Engineering Laboratory, 1940　　　　$2.75
Ideaphoria *by Johnson O'Connor*
Human Engineering Laboratory, 1944　　　　$4.00

The Laboratory's mathematical techniques

Psychometrics *by Johnson O'Connor*
Harvard University Press, 1934　　　　$3.50

Out of print

Born That Way *by Johnson O'Connor*
Williams and Wilkins, 1928

VOCABULARY TEST FORMS

Applicable fifth grade to second year high school.
Junior English Vocabulary, Worksample 176, Form BA
Applicable first year high school through college.

English Vocabulary, Worksample 95, Form AD
English Vocabulary, Worksample 95, Form BC
English Vocabulary, Worksample 95, Form CC
English Vocabulary, Worksample 95, Form DB
English Vocabulary, Worksample 95, Form EB
Ten dollars per ten copies. Single copies not sold.

TECHNICAL REPORTS

Accounting Aptitude

Number

9 Word-Checking Test, Worksample 43 (1936) (out of print)

31 Preliminary Norms for the Checking-Series Test, Worksample 223 by Mary O. Luqueer (1939)

68 Analysis of Time and Errors in Relation to Reliability of Two Clerical Tests, Worksample 1 and Worksample 223 by Robert G. Barnum (1940)

78 Development of a Generally Applicable Norm Scale for Clerical Worksamples on the Basis of Median Ratio Scores by Samuel P. Horton (1941)

79 Construction of Four Clerical Tests, Worksamples 267, 268, 269, and 270 by Robert G. Barnum (1941)

Art Appreciation

23 Factors in the Art Appreciation Test, Worksample 172 by Samuel P. Horton (1939)

44 Two Experiments in the Simplification of the Measure of Art Appraisal by Samuel P. Horton (1939)

Behavior

6 Revision of Form A of Worksample 169, Judgment in Social Situations (1936)

15 Statistical and Graphic Analysis of Three Forms of Worksample 169, Judgment in Social Situations (1938)

Creative Imagination

45 Experiments in the Scoring of a Measure of Creative Imagination, Worksample 161 by Samuel P. Horton (1940)

49 Integrated Norms, Forms BA, G, and H, for the Creative-Imagination Test, Worksample 161 by Florence E. Hauck (1940)

56 Separate Norms for Eight Test Administrators—A Study in Testing Technique, Worksample 161 by Samuel P. Horton (1940)

71 Relative Accuracy of Group and Individual Testing Techniques for the Creative-Imagination Test, Worksample 161 by Samuel P. Horton (1940)

Dexterity

16 Administration and Norms for the Finger-Dexterity Test, Worksample 16, and the Tweezer-Dexterity Test, Worksample 18 by Florence E. Hauck (1938)

88 Application of the Median-Ratio Technique for Two Non-clerical Speed Tests by Samuel P. Horton (1942)

93 New Scoring Scale for Tweezer Dexterity, Worksample 18, and Related Research by R. Birnie Horgan (1941)

Discrimination

61 Statistical Analysis of Five Discrimination Tests by Mary O. Luqueer (1940)

86 Analysis Leading to a Proposed Revision of the Pitch-Discrimination Test, Worksample 76 by Charles R. Wilks (1940)

Discrimination (Continued)

English Vocabulary (Continued)

Judgment

Knowledge of Painting

Left Sidedness

Memory

Observation

Proportion Appraisal

Reasoning

Reasoning (Continued)

Number

110 Analysis of the Inductive-Reasoning Test, Worksample 164, as to Internal Consistency and Relation to Clerical Test, Worksample 1 *by William H. Helme* (1943)

111 A Study of the Relationship between Inductive Reasoning, Worksample 164 FA and Number Checking, Worksample 268 *by Mary O. Luqueer* (1943)

Structural Visualization

13 The Formboard, Worksample 173, as a Mental Measure (1937)

14 An Analysis of the First Trial of the Black Cube, Worksample 167 (1938)

18 An Analysis of the Second Trial of the Black Cube, Worksample 167 (1938)

19 Methods of Computing Practice Factors (1938)

25 An Analysis of the Pyramid, Worksample 68 *by Samuel P. Horton* (1938)

26 The Relation of Assembly Test Practice Factors to Age and Sex *by Florence E. Hauck* (1938)

47 First Experiment with the Graded Series of Black Cube Tests *by Samuel P. Horton* (1940)

65 Revised Norms and Age Factors for the Graded Wiggly Blocks, Worksamples 4 and 5 *by Florence E. Hauck* (1940)

69 Conversion of Worksample 4 Scores to Permit the Use of a Single Norm Table for Worksamples 4 and 5, Graded Wiggly Blocks *by Florence E. Hauck* (1940)

Tapping

39 Reliability and Norms for the Tapping Test, Worksample 221 *by Samuel P. Horton* (1939)

40 Preliminary Study of the Fatigue and Practice Effects on the Tapping Test, Worksample 221, Form A *by Mary O. Luqueer* (1939)

Technical Vocabularies

7 The Physics Technical Vocabulary, Worksample 181 (1936)

20 Revision of Form C of the Physics Technical Vocabulary, Worksample 181 *by Russell E. Sprague* (1938)

50 Vocabulary of Wines and Liquors, Worksample 290, Form A *by Frank L. McLanathan* (1939)

85 The Construction of the Vocabulary of Music, Worksample 295, Form A *by Frank L. McLanathan* (1941)

92 The Construction of the Vocabulary of Medicine, Worksample 323, Form A *by Mary E. Filley* (1942)

Validation

1 Characteristics of Graduate Nurses (1934)

2 The English Vocabulary Scores of 75 Executives (1935) (out of print)

4 Comparative Scores of Two Groups of Graduate Nurses (1935) (out of print)

8 A Two-Year Follow-up of Student Nurses (1936)

17 First Analysis of the Traits of Fifty-six Secondary School Boys (1937)

Number

27 Preliminary Study of 20 Problem Students *by Margaret E. Ferry* (1938)

46 Relationships Among Nineteen Group Tests and Their Validity for Freshmen Engineering Marks *by Samuel P. Horton* (1939)

75 Conversion of College Entrance Rating Scale Words into Their Genus and Species of the Residues of Vilfredo Pareto *by H. A. Zantow* (1940)

77 An Analysis of the Scores of Eight Stock-Traders *by Evelyn C. Wight* (1941)

81 Report I—Analysis of the Worksample Scores of Forty-nine Accountants; Report II—Follow-up of Twenty-five Accountants; Report III—Composite Scoring Scale for Number Checking and Wiggly Block, Worksamples 1 and 5 *by Leonard C. Seeley* (1940)

90 An Analysis of the Worksample Scores of 101 High-School Teachers *by Leonard C. Seeley* (1941)

96 Analysis of the Worksample Scores of Seventy-six Educational Advisers in the Civilian Conservation Corps *by Leonard C. Seeley* (1941)

97 A Follow-up of the Careers of Tested Engineering Students—Volume I—(A Preliminary Survey of the Test Scores of Groups Classified by Their Records in the Educational Phase of Their Careers) *by Samuel P. Horton* (1941); Volume II—(Occupational Success of 203 Men in Relation to Their Test Scores Obtained When They Were Students) *by Samuel P. Horton* (1942); Volume III—(A Continuation of the Study of the Occupational Careers of 203 Men to Test Scores Obtained from Them as Students) *by Samuel P. Horton* (1943)

100 Preliminary Report on a Statistical Study of the Stevens Defense Industries School Group—1st Session *by Samuel P. Horton* (1942)

101 Analysis of the Worksample Scores of 109 Engineers *by Leonard C. Seeley* (1942)

102 Preliminary Study of the Relationship of Test Scores to Success or Failure in School *by Mary O. Luqueer* (1942)

107 Report to the U. S. War Department on Tests for Trainability in the War Industries Training School *by Samuel P. Horton* (1942)

113 A Study of the Correlations between Worksamples 1, 4, and 5, 16, 18, and 35 AE with High School Subjects *by Katherine J. Rippere* (1943)

Each, two dollars.
All of these may be obtained through the
Human Engineering Laboratory
347 Beacon Street, Boston, Massachusetts.